the essential

·

—— guide *to* ——

·

natural

·

SKIN

·

CARE

ABOUT THE AUTHOR

Hélène Berton (Quebec, Canada) has been working with essential oils since 2000. Her training includes an apprenticeship at an artisanal distillery in Provence. She regularly gives workshops on natural cosmetics and related topics.

the essential

guide *to*

natural

SKIN

CARE

Choosing

Botanicals,

Oils, *&* Extracts

for Simple

& Healthy

Beauty

Hélène Berton

Llewellyn Publications
Woodbury, Minnesota

First Edition
First Printing, 2012

First published in French in 2006 as *Les huiles essentielles pour la peau: Une saine alternative cosmétique: huiles végétales, beurres végétaux, extraits oléiques, huiles essentielles, hydrolats aromatiques*, by the publishing house Aroleome éditeur and again in 2008 as *Les huiles essentielles pour la peau: Une saine alternative cosmétique: huiles végétales, beurres végétaux, extraits oléiques, huiles essentielles, hydrolats aromatiques* by the publishing house Éditions Favre.

Cover art: Background © iStockphoto.com/studiovision,
    Leaves © iStockphoto.com/Nishan Sothilingam
Cover design by Kevin R. Brown
Translated from French by Patricia Watt

Llewellyn Publications is a registered trademark of Llewellyn Worldwide Ltd.

Library of Congress Cataloging-in-Publication Data
Berton, Helene, 1963–
  [Huiles essentielles pour la peau. English]
  The essential guide to natural skin care : choosing botanicals, oils &
extracts for simple & healthy beauty / by Helene Berton. — 1st ed.
    p. cm.
  Includes bibliographical references and index.
  ISBN 978-0-7387-2927-5
  1. Skin—Care and hygiene. 2. Essences and essential oils. 3.
Aromatherapy. 4. Cosmetics. I. Title.
  RL87.B47 2012
  646.7'26—dc23

                                                          2011049556

Llewellyn Worldwide Ltd. does not participate in, endorse, or have any authority or responsibility concerning private business transactions between our authors and the public.
    All mail addressed to the author is forwarded, but the publisher cannot, unless specifically instructed by the author, give out an address or phone number.
    Any Internet references contained in this work are current at publication time, but the publisher cannot guarantee that a specific location will continue to be maintained. Please refer to the publisher's website for links to authors' websites and other sources.

Llewellyn Publications
A Division of Llewellyn Worldwide Ltd.
2143 Wooddale Drive
Woodbury, MN 55125-2989
www.llewellyn.com

Printed in the United States of America

CONTENTS

Part Three
THE APPENDICES

The reader must keep in mind that the presence of any symptom, minor or severe, requires medical advice.

Preface

I have enjoyed the world of plants since I was a child. I will never forget the wonderful garden at my paternal grandparents' house in France. I played there when I was very young. What attracted me most were the flowers—their perfumes and colors, as well as the many types of fruit that grew in the garden, which I sampled to my heart's content. I loved to pluck leaves from the huge laurel tree that grew beside the house; then I would crease the leaves and breathe in deeply to smell their powerful aroma. I must confess, however, that the multitude of vegetables that my grandfather grew left me rather indifferent. Later, my mother stimulated my interest in nature, especially my interest in the plant world.

It was during my adolescence that the properties and virtues of medicinal plants began to attract my attention, and it was then that I started to experiment. Before it became the fashion, I would prepare salads that included daisies and nasturtium for our family suppers. I concocted all sorts of herbal teas. And I would rinse my hair with an infusion made from fresh nettle leaves.

Though life has led me to study and work in other domains, I have always kept my great interest in plants. I am still fascinated by their powers and the benefits we can obtain from them.

In the year 2000, a friend introduced me to essential oils. It was like falling in love. Since then, these precious substances have been my daily companions—serving as therapeutic ingredients and as ingredients for skin and hair care products.

A little later, after reading several books and performing many experiments, I wanted to learn about aromatherapy in order to better understand essential oils and to master their use. During this training, I discovered vegetable oils, vegetable butters, infused oils, and aromatic hydrosols (water-based solutions created when essential oils are distilled), and came to understand how they complement each other. After creating my first successful skin care recipe, I started using my own preparations and stopped using commercial products. Then I took workshops to learn how to produce a variety of natural skin and hair care products.

My apprenticeship continued, enriched by more readings, experiments, conferences, and seminars—including those given by world-renowned specialist and researcher Pierre Franchomme. I also did a sort of apprenticeship at an artisanal distillery in Provence in order to learn firsthand how to gather and distill aromatic plants. In addition, I discussed the subject with several friends, who are as passionate about it as I am. Each time I prepare a new edition of this book (first in Quebec in French, and then in Switzerland, and now in English for North America), I integrate new information and details I have learned since the previous edition.

At first, it was by instinct that I chose to use the natural substances that are presented in this book. I enjoy their fine, satiny texture on my fingers, and the variety of their aromas—light or powerful, flowery, fruity, or green—depending on which plant they come from. In addition to their beneficial effects, I love the sensation of softness and freshness that they leave on my skin. Furthermore, I find them very easy to use.

Rita Stiens's book *La vérité sur les cosmétiques (The Truth about Cosmetics)* led me to understand that these natural substances are an excellent alternative to commercial products. Ms. Stiens has thrown light on the dubious practices of many professionals in the skin and hair care industry. In fact, certain companies have no scruples about offering products that have little effect—or, indeed, a detrimental effect—on our health in the long term. Furthermore, they have few legal obligations to provide information about the ingredients they use. And all this in the name of profit.

Several years ago, I stopped buying creams, milk, and toners. Now I only use vegetable oils, vegetable butters, essential oils, infused oils, and hydrosols on my face, body, hands, lips, and hair. Over time, I have widened my range of ingredients, and refined and diversified my formulas. When I prepare my directions, I always aim for simplicity and efficiency, carefully choosing the most appropriate ingredients for the effect I am seeking. As a bonus, this costs me considerably less than the commercial products.

My skin has become softer, and my complexion has become clearer. Vegetable oils penetrate well and nourish the skin thoroughly. I never have a greasy film on my face, even in summer. Some ingredients allow me to eliminate or control the blemishes that appear on my face from time to time. My preparations for the hands, legs, and body leave my skin soft in all seasons. My hair is softer and silkier. The friends and acquaintances to whom I have offered my products have greatly appreciated their beneficial effects. I even had a pleasant surprise. After a year of using my facial care oil, the scar I have had on my forehead since I was a little girl had been remarkably reduced. Now it can hardly be seen.

Like many women, I do not have the peaches-and-cream complexion that so many seem to dream about. The ingredients that I use, just like the commercial beauty products, cannot make the wrinkles that have come with time completely disappear. It's a law of nature. I don't know what the state of my skin would be if I had continued to use the classic skin care products. In any case, I doubt that my skin would be in better condition than it is today.

Every time I wanted to develop a new preparation, I had to dig into several books. I didn't always find what I was looking for. Some books would give good recipes, but would give only partial information about the ingredients. Other times, it was the opposite. Certain ingredients that I find of great interest do not appear in any reference book about natural skin and hair care products and aromatherapy. Because of these experiences, I gradually came up with the idea of this book— a reference guide for natural skin and hair care products that would include simple recipes as well as complete and precise information about quality ingredients that are easy to use and really effective.

This book is meant for people who already have a basic knowledge of essential oils or homemade skin care products. While some recipes such as skin care oils are very simple to make and to use, most of the others require some basic familiarity with the ingredients and the preparations presented here. Those who have a good background of prior experience with making their own products can even skip the section on preparations in Part One.

This book consists of three parts. Part One gives an overview of current practices and legal obligations in the skin and hair care industry. It will help you to better understand the ingredients contained in the products that are widely available (including those that are labeled natural and organic). It explains the nature of various ingredients, their advantages and disadvantages, and in certain cases, how they can be harmful. It will help you make better-informed choices when you are buying commercial products, rather than blindly following the advertising of the manufacturers. It contains recipes for healthy-alternative skin and hair care products that rely on natural vegetable ingredients. The recipes are easy to follow and include example quantities. Using these recipes, you can prepare your own skin care oils, toners, and ointments, as well as oils and preparations for hair care, lip balms, and other lotions and creams that are of the finest quality and personalized to your needs and tastes.

Part Two describes the general characteristics of the ingredients mentioned elsewhere in the book. It explains their nature and origin, as well as how they are produced. It also includes detailed explanations of their properties relating to skin and hair care, gives advice on when and how to use them, and provides any other pertinent information. This reference section will allow you to choose among the **thirty-four vegetable oils**, **seven vegetable butters**, **six infused oils**, **thirty-two essential oils**, **twenty-one hydrosols**, and **nine emulsifiers** that are described.

The third and final part of the book contains a number of appendices that index the ingredients in different ways. Appendix 1 groups the ingredients according to their properties. Appendix 2 groups the ingredients based on recommended usage. The final three appendices list the French, English, and Latin names of the plants cited throughout the book. Finally, a bibliography provides a list of references in the fields of aromatherapy, vegetable oils, natural skin and hair care products, and medicinal plants.

Bring this book to the health food or specialized stores when shopping for ingredients, or use it at home to make different recipes for each member of your family, depending on his or her skin type.

I hope that it lives up to your expectations and that you will have a fascinating adventure in the world of oils.

Hélène Berton
Aroma enthusiast

Acknowledgments

My sincerest thanks to André, Claude, Clotilde, Delphine, Emmanuel, Hiêp, François, Isabelle, Laurence, Lucie, Patricia, and Thérèse.

Your encouragement, questions, comments, advice, and suggestions have been a real contribution to the realization of this book.

part

ONE

Skin and

Hair Care

Products

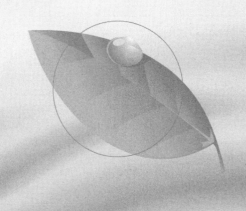

The Skin and Hair Care Industry

The number of skin and hair care products on the market is astronomical. And the skin and hair care industry is flourishing.

Whether you are looking for a miracle product that will allow you to keep an eternally youthful appearance or simply want to maintain your hair and skin, you are a consumer of skin and hair care products. Manufacturers of beauty products all surf skillfully on the ever-increasing demand for their products with ever-greater advertising promises. They go to great lengths to keep our attention on their miraculous creations.

Not subject to the type of strict controls governing certain industries, such as pharmaceuticals, manufacturers of beauty products can include a panoply of synthetic chemicals in their products. These ingredients give the products, among other qualities, a silky appearance, pleasing perfumes, and attractive colors, as well as a long shelf life. Indeed, these characteristics seem to have a higher priority than effectiveness or the long-term safety of our health.

THE INCI DECLARATION

In a number of countries, manufacturers of beauty products are still not required to declare the composition of their products on containers and packaging. Some jurisdictions, however, have decided to address the lack of transparency in this area. The United States, Canada, the members of the European Union, Japan, and Australia, for example, all now require a list of ingredients on skin and hair care products.

To this end, all these countries have adopted *INCI*—the *International Nomenclature of Cosmetic Ingredients*. It is a multilingual dictionary that serves as a common reference for all participating countries. Product ingredients must now appear on containers or packaging. Natural ingredients are listed by their Latin names and synthetic ingredients by their technical names. Ingredients must be listed in the order of their percentage in the product—from largest to smallest, using their INCI-approved Latin or technical names.

While INCI is a significant step in the right direction, this legal requirement to declare ingredients using the specified naming conventions has the following shortcomings:

- The list of ingredients is often printed in tiny characters, which makes it difficult to read (even before 40 years of age).

- The terminology used is rather esoteric for the general population. It does not require the form in which the ingredient is included (extract, powder, refined, raw), nor the method used to extract or produce the ingredient (chemical solvents and so on).

- Colorants are only indicated by a code.
- Ingredients that constitute less than 1% of the product can be listed in any order regardless of their quantity.
- All countries do not apply the same rules. For example, Europe requires that potentially allergenic substances in perfumes and fragrances must be indicated. Other countries do not have such a requirement.

Often, the shorter the list of INCI ingredients, the better. Manufacturers of products that are made from natural primary materials often include fewer additives. This greatly reduces the list of ingredients.

The regulations are not perfect. Nonetheless, they make it possible to detect the presence of certain ingredients that appear more often and whose safety is becoming more dubious, especially if they are used daily on a long-term basis. The ingredients list reveals a lot more about the quality of a product than its price and other information that may be provided on the bottle—which unfortunately are not good indicators of the actual value of the contents.

COMMON INGREDIENTS

Health Canada defines a cosmetic product as "any substance or mixture of substances, manufactured, sold or represented for the purpose of cleansing, improving or altering the complexion, skin, hair, or teeth, including deodorants and perfumes." A large proportion of these products are creams and milks used for facial and body care. These products are composed of an active ingredient, an excipient (an inert substance that serves as a vehicle for the active ingredient), and additional substances (or adjuvants).

In advertising, manufacturers of these products often put the emphasis on the *active ingredients*. They constantly use the terms "new," "revolutionary," "innovative," and "scientific research." What they fail to tell us is that these active ingredients only represent a minute percentage of the product, sometimes as little as 0.1%, as Rita Stiens, the author of *La vérité sur les cosmetiques (The Truth About Cosmetics)*, states. The beneficial effects of these ingredients are not always as real or as visible as the manufacturer claims. They are responsible for, at most, 20% of the effectiveness of the product.

The *excipient* is the main component of a skin care product that carries the product's active ingredient to the skin. In the case of creams and milks, the excipient is an emulsion, which is often called the "mayonnaise" in the jargon of the professionals. An emulsion is a mixture of two liquids, typically water (or a water-based liquid) and oil (or an oil-based liquid). The two liquids are kept in suspension by one or more emulsifiers. An emulsifier is a substance that links the two liquids in a stable way. Emulsifiers create a smooth mixture—like the egg yolk in mayonnaise. The excipient (into which the active ingredients are incorporated) is the main component of skin care milks and creams. In most commercial products, the excipient is a neutral substance that does not have any beneficial properties for the skin.

In general, the oil component of an excipient (the basic emulsion) is a mineral oil derived from petroleum, such as liquid paraffin. Mineral oils are used because they are cheap, stable, colorless, and odorless. Not only do they not nourish the skin, but they block the pores and prevent the skin from breathing. Silicon oils, which are used in some products, are also harmful for the environment because they are not very biodegradable. As for aqueous components, they are usually based on distilled water, and are usually the first ingredient in the INCI listing. Last but not least, emulsifiers are usually synthetic chemicals.

As can be seen from its composition, the excipient adds no cosmetic value to the product. Instead it can be harmful to the skin and to the body as a whole.

According to Rita Stiens, the excipient represents about 90% of the product in terms of quantity, and should contribute 80% of its effectiveness, regardless of which active ingredient it is delivering. Therefore, a good excipient, composed of high-quality aqueous or oil ingredients, will result in a good product that is able to nourish and protect the skin. Conversely, a cosmetic product whose excipient consists of mediocre or even harmful ingredients can never really be effective or beneficial for the skin.

Popular cosmetic products are designed to have a shelf life of two to three years, even before you open them and start using them. In order to prevent the development of the bacteria and fungi associated with rancidity, preservatives and antioxidants are added. Because of their powerful antibacterial action, certain preservatives also destroy the bacterial flora that naturally protects the skin. Recent studies have tended to show that certain preservatives—such as those derived from formaldehydes, parabens, and phthalates—pass through the skin barrier and enter the body. Among other side effects, some preservatives can be carcinogenic and can provoke an increase in estrogen production by the body.

Some industrial skin and hair care products also contain a number of additional substances that are produced by chemical synthesis. This is the case for perfumes, colorants, moisturizers, softeners, thickeners, stabilizers, solvents, sunscreens, and so on. Some of these irritate the skin and can cause allergic reactions.

The National Institute for Occupational Safety and Health, which protects the health and security of American workers, has noted that of the chemical ingredients used in cosmetic products, 884 are toxic. Very little reliable scientific data is available on the interaction among these ingredients and the effects these mixtures have on the human body. And this does not take into account all the substances that have not been the subject of long-term studies. INCI includes more than 12,000 natural and synthetic ingredients used in cosmetics.

Public authorities, both national and international (including the World Health Organization), are examining the nature and security of these ingredients more and more closely. Unfortunately, many ingredients currently used in commercial products are far from innocuous. For example, manufacturers who use ingredients that have been declared toxic benefit from a certain delay before the ingredients are formally banned. This allows them to use up their stocks. Some manufacturers have found a way to get around the quantity limits that can be set on ingredients: they simply increase the number of ingredients. For example, in a certain product, they may use seven preservatives (each of which has a quantity limit) rather than just two. Each of the seven ingredients is present in such a minute quantity that it will be allowed and only mentioned at the bottom of the list of ingredients. But the result is the same with regard to the total quantity of synthetic preservatives and the potential toxicity of the product.

We know that the skin absorbs up to 60% of the substances that are applied to it (and that the rest returns to the environment).

NATURAL SKIN AND HAIR CARE PRODUCTS

The word "natural" is not defined in the law of any land nor in the charter of any organization. In products labeled "natural," we may find exactly the same types of ingredients as those present in other products that do not have this label.

The substances, to which a manufacturer may be referring in order to justify the label "natural," could just as easily be water or alcohol as a plant extract. And, even when an ingredient is based on or extracted from a plant, there is no guarantee of its quality. You can find many creams that contain shea butter (a vegetable butter with excellent cosmetic properties) that show no sign of its color or aroma. These creams penetrate the skin immediately, leaving no greasy feeling, and do not go rancid when they are exposed to air for a certain amount of time. This indicates not only that the amount of shea butter used is minimal, but also that the shea butter that is present was probably refined to the detriment of its real dermocosmetic properties.

Example INCI declaration

"Distilled water, stearic acid, glycerine, liquid paraffin, glycerol monostearate, dimethyl silicone oil, potassium hydroxide, fragrance, carbomer resin, methyl-p-hydroxybenzoate, propyl para-hydroxy-benzoate, methyl, FD&C Red No. 3, FD&C Yellow No. 5."

Apart from water, stearic acid, and perhaps glycerine, this product is entirely composed of synthetic chemical ingredients. The manufacturer (who produces a popular brand of skin and hair care products that are distributed internationally) includes the words "aromatherapy" and "citrus-ginger" on the bottle. The back of the bottle also states that "this lotion was created following the principles of aromatherapy whose aim is to improve health and well-being through the use of aromas."

Another common strategy is to include a natural active ingredient of an acceptable quality, but in a minimal quantity, in an excipient composed of commonly used synthetic ingredients like paraffin oil. What is the value of such a product?

Some manufacturers stretch the idea of natural even further when they use the terms "plant extracts" or "essential oils." When one reads the INCI declaration, one realizes that these terms are often being used to describe synthetic perfumes.

The use of the term "natural source" is also questionable. It is often used to refer to components that were obtained in a raw form from nature, but were extracted using chemical processes or were transformed in some way. We do not know exactly how they were processed and with what result.

In short, the term "natural" is not well defined and does not guarantee the quality of the product with which it is associated.

CERTIFIED ORGANIC SKIN AND HAIR CARE PRODUCTS

Faced with the lax approach of government authorities with respect to the ingredients used in the skin and hair care industry, various organic certification organizations, especially in Europe, have established strict standards for cosmetic ingredients. The purpose of these standards is to assure basic quality for consumers.

A manufacturer whose product has been certified by one of these organizations must state the name of the certifying organization on the product label beside the term "organic." This name is extremely important, since it allows one to know to which standard the manufacturer is conforming.

Generally speaking, all these certifying organizations ban ingredients derived from petroleum (paraffin oil, glycols, etc.) and from animals (other than those naturally produced by the animals themselves, such as honey, beeswax, milk, etc.), as well as synthetic perfumes and colorants, silicon, and toxic preservatives. They impose strict standards with respect to quality and processing of the ingredients that they approve, and the products that they certify.

These certification bodies are a great improvement in the quality assurance of organic skin and hair care products. But a product that is certified organic is not necessarily composed entirely of ingredients that are themselves certified organic and totally harmless. Thus, ingredients derived from plants and those naturally produced by animals do not all have to be organic. And a number of natural ingredients that have been chemically transformed (esterified vegetable oils, surfactants, emulsifiers, etc.) are also authorized. It is difficult to find information about their characteristics and the exact processes used to produce them.

Furthermore, each certifying organization has its own standards. Some are less strict than others. The standards are sometimes difficult to obtain. Not so long ago, one certification organization was selling its standards to the public for about $125, and now they are only available to its members. And the standards are not always easy to decipher—especially for the layperson.

Certified organic products are sold, on average, for 30% more than equivalent products that are not certified. It is important to be well informed and to read the labels carefully rather than blindly choosing the first product you see simply because it is certified organic.

BEYOND SKIN AND HAIR CARE PRODUCTS

The best skin care product cannot overcome certain undeniable facts. The skin (and the hair) is primarily maintained and nourished by the nutritive substances delivered by the blood. Lifestyle habits are thus reflected in it.

- A healthy, balanced diet, exercise, good oxygenation, and adequate sleep (both in quality and quantity) will all have beneficial effects.

- On the other hand, too much alcohol or tobacco, dietary abuse, and overexposure to sun or cold will all be harmful.

- Exposure to excessive stress that is badly managed can have an impact.

- Morphology also has an impact: high cheekbones and a strong chin support the skin better.

- Genes also play a role: they partly predetermine skin quality and the rate at which the skin ages.

- Finally, plumper people will have skin that is tauter and less wrinkled than thin people.

Two

A Healthy Alternative for Skin and Hair Care Products

INTRODUCTION

As mentioned in the previous chapter, the quality of a dermo-cosmetic product is almost entirely dependent on the quality of the ingredients in the excipient. After that comes the quality of the active ingredients.

Vegetable oils, vegetable butters, infused oils, and hydrosols are all perfect ingredients for emulsions and simple preparations that nourish, protect, and repair the skin. Essential oils, when carefully selected, are excellent active ingredients. When they are of good quality, these are the ingredients of choice for skin and hair care products. They have always been used in traditional beauty products. The use of rich and nourishing ingredients in the excipient can lay to rest the false ideas that the excipient must be a neutral, valueless medium and that only the active ingredients determine the quality and effectiveness of the product. Part Two of this book describes these ingredients in detail.

With the Turn of the Seasons

In winter, when the air and the skin become drier, it is preferable to use preparations composed of richer oils that can nourish the skin better. During the summer, it is better to use products based on oils and butters that are more fluid, and can, therefore, penetrate the skin more quickly.

Oils from fruit seeds and pits are a good use of the waste material resulting from the production of syrups, jams, juices and other drinks, and fruit pastes.

Many natural ingredients from vegetable, animal, and mineral sources (such as algae, mink oil, and clay) have very attractive cosmetic properties. However, this book focuses on ingredients that have these advantages:

- They are easy to obtain, for the most part.

- They are easy to store, preserve, and transport (if you follow certain simple rules).

- If they are stored in good conditions, they last a long time (one to two years for certain hydrosols, longer for most vegetable oils and butters, and several years for most essential oils).

- They can be used simply on a daily basis, and they can also be adapted for use in more complex preparations.

- They do not contribute to the suffering of animals.

- They are a source of environmentally friendly income for people in developing countries. For example, shea butter and argan oil, which are very popular, constitute a valuable source of supplementary income for the people of sub-Saharan Africa and Morocco, and, in some cases, are their only source of income.

- They are an environmentally friendly choice because they reinforce the demand for unrefined products cultivated without synthetic fertilizer. They offer a commercially viable alternative for farmers who want to use ecological methods rather than intensive, industrialized agriculture. They do not release toxic products into the environment, because they simply do not contain any toxic products.

- The use of certain ingredients may actually promote the conservation of plant species, especially those that have a new commercial value, as long as they are not overharvested. Unfortunately, some wild plants, such Indian sandalwood, are being overexploited.

You might think that making your own cosmetic products is complicated and difficult. This not always true. Apart from emulsions, many preparations are very easy and involve very little manipulation. By preparing your own products, you can have products of the highest quality at a very reasonable cost. It simply involves choosing the best ingredients for the product you want to make, which depends on your needs and the effects that you are seeking.

The rest of Part One is devoted to descriptions of the various types of products that you can make. It includes basic recipes and examples, as well as explanations of how to use them, and their advantages and disadvantages.

SKIN CARE OILS

Skin care oils consist of a vegetable oil or a mixture of vegetable oils to which essential oils have been added. Since some vegetable oils are very fluid and penetrate very well, this type of preparation suits all skin types.

The basic formula for a skin care oil is:

- 100% vegetable oil (or infused oil)
- A few drops of essential oil:
  - 0.5 to 1% for an ordinary preparation (or 5 to 10 drops of essential oil for 1 ounce of vegetable oil)
  - 2 to 4% for a therapeutic preparation (for acne, couperosis, etc.) (or 20 to 40 drops of essential oil for 1 ounce of vegetable oil)

To prepare the oil, mix the ingredients in a small bottle made of tinted glass with a plastic eye-dropper lid (cut the inner part of the dropper to let the preparation drip out more easily). You can keep this small bottle on your bathroom counter (away from direct sunlight) for daily use, as long as you prepared only the quantity you'll need for one or two months. If you made a larger batch, keep a small bottle of it in the bathroom and keep the rest of your preparation in the refrigerator.

To use the oil, put a few drops in the palm of your hand, then apply it to the skin and massage it in gently until it is absorbed.

For facial skin care, a 10 ml (⅓ fl. oz.) bottle will last about four weeks, depending on how much your skin absorbs it. Because of the small quantities involved, you can easily adjust the proportions used for the vegetable oils and the essential oils to suit your needs.

If you want to make a body oil, increase the quantities up to 50 ml (1⅔ fl. oz.) to 100 ml (3⅓ fl. oz.) of vegetable oil and adjust the amount of essential oils according to the basic formula presented above.

Sample Recipes

Oil for Oily Skin

10 ml (⅓ fl. oz.)	Jojoba vegetable oil
2 drops	Petitgrain bigarade essential oil
1 drop	Clary sage essential oil

Oil for Skin Prone to Couperosis

5 ml (⅙ fl. oz.)	Tamanu vegetable oil
5 ml (⅙ fl. oz.)	Musk rose oil
5 drops	Helichrysum essential oil
5 drops	Cypress essential oil

Skin care oil is very easy to prepare, to bottle, and to use. It keeps very well because it does not contain any water-based ingredients in which bacteria and fungus can develop. It is an easy way to become familiar with vegetable oils and essential oils. It will allow you to identify which oils suit you (as much for their aroma and texture as for their effect on your skin) before you jump into making more complex preparations. It is really the simplest, healthiest, and most effective alternative cosmetic.

TONERS

Rich in plant extracts, true hydrosols are excellent for skin and hair care. If handled and stored properly, they are free from bacteria. They keep very well. You can use hydrosols as is, or you can combine several to create a custom toner. Usually sold in a spray bottle, hydrosols require no special handling if they are not mixed together.

Sample Recipes

Toner for Sensitive Skin

25 ml (⅚ fl. oz.)   Roman chamomile hydrosol
25 ml (⅚ fl. oz.)   Rose hydrosol

Toner for Skin Prone to Acne

30 ml (1 fl. oz.)   Rosemary ct verbenone hydrosol
10 ml (⅓ fl. oz.)   True lavender hydrosol
10 ml (⅓ fl. oz.)   Lemon Balm hydrosol

To use, lightly mist your face with the spray bottle (about 4–6 small sprays). The toner may be kept on a bathroom counter (away from direct sunlight) for daily use. A 50 ml (1⅔ oz.) bottle will last one to two months. If you purchased or mixed a larger amount, put some in a smaller spray bottle and keep the rest of it in the refrigerator.

OINTMENTS

Ointments are like creams, but are made from oils and butters only. They do not include an aqueous phase, and, therefore, are not emulsions. Particular proportions of solid and liquid fats give ointments their special soft consistency, which makes them easy to spread. Beeswax can be included in an ointment to add its thickening, softening, and protective properties.

Since ointments contain a significant amount of vegetable butter, they are very rich and suitable for dry and normal skin rather than oily skin. By choosing light vegetable oils and butters that easily penetrate the skin, the ointment will have a very nice, less greasy texture.

The basic formula for an ointment is:

- 50% vegetable butter
- 45% vegetable oil (or infused oil)
- 5% beeswax
- A few drops of essential oil:
  - 0.5 to 1% for an ordinary preparation (or 5 to 10 drops of essential oil for 1 ounce of ointment)
  - 2 to 4% for a therapeutic preparation (for acne, couperosis, etc.) (or 20 to 40 drops of essential oil for 1 ounce of ointment)

or

- 60% vegetable butter
- 40% vegetable oil (or infused oil)
- A few drops of essential oil:

- 0.5 to 1% for an ordinary preparation (or 5 to 10 drops of essential oil for 1 ounce of ointment)
- 2 to 4% for a therapeutic preparation (for acne, couperosis, etc.) (or 20 to 40 drops of essential oil for 1 ounce of ointment)

or

- 88% vegetable oil (or infused oil)
- 12% beeswax
- A few drops of essential oil:
  - 0.5 to 1% for an ordinary preparation (or 5 to 10 drops of essential oil for 1 ounce of ointment)
  - 2 to 4% for a therapeutic preparation (for acne, couperosis, etc.) (or 20 to 40 drops of essential oil for 1 ounce of ointment)

If you use a very firm butter (for example, cocoa butter), you can slightly reduce the amount of butter and slightly increase the amount of vegetable oil.

To prepare an ointment, melt the butter and/or beeswax in a double boiler, then add the oil or infused oil, and mix well. Take the mixture off the double boiler and when it starts to cool and slightly thicken, add the essential oil. Pour the mixture into small jars made of tinted glass. Allow the ointment to cool completely and solidify before using.

Sample Recipes
Ointment for Dry Skin

30 g (1 oz.)	Mango butter
10 ml (⅓ fl. oz.)	Sesame vegetable oil

| 10 ml (⅓ fl. oz.) | Calendula infused oil |
| 15 drops | Palmarosa essential oil |

Ointment for Dry Hands with Pigmentation Spots

25 g (⅚ oz.)	Shea butter
11 ml (⅓ fl. oz.)	Castor vegetable oil
11 ml (⅓ fl. oz.)	Comfrey infused oil
3 g (.1 oz)	Beeswax
20 drops	Carrot essential oil
25 drops	Celery essential oil

Starch can also be added to an ointment—up to 10% of the total weight. The starch can be cornstarch, rice starch, arrowroot, or any fine starch of plant origin. The starch can be in powder or pulverized crystal form. Starch will give the ointment a satiny texture and make it less greasy to the touch. Add the starch when mixing the ingredients in the double boiler.

Ointments are easy to prepare. Bacteria and mold cannot grow in ointments because they do not contain water or any aqueous ingredients. Ointments can, however, turn rancid if they are exposed to air, light, or heat, and if they are left unused for a long time (a natural result of the oxidation process for all fats).

Keep a small tinted-glass jar of ointment on the bathroom counter (away from direct sunlight) for daily use with a quantity equal to one to two months' use, but not more. If a larger quantity was made, keep the remaining ointment in other jars in the refrigerator.

HAIR CARE PREPARATIONS

Hair care preparations are composed of vegetable oils and butters (some vegetable oils, such as jojoba, are very gentle, even for oily hair). They are applied to the hair before washing, and are left on for two hours or more.

The basic formula for a hair care preparation is:

- 100% vegetable oil (or infused oil)
- A few drops of essential oil:
  - 0.5 to 1% for an ordinary preparation (or 5 to 10 drops of essential oil for 1 ounce of preparation)
  - 2 to 4% for a therapeutic preparation (for dandruff, hair loss, etc.) (or 20 to 40 drops of essential oil for 1 ounce of preparation)

or

- 70% vegetable oil (or infused oil)
- 30% vegetable butter
- A few drops of essential oil:
  - 0.5 to 1% for an ordinary preparation (or 5 to 10 drops of essential oil for 1 ounce of preparation)
  - 2 to 4% for a therapeutic preparation (for dandruff, hair loss, etc.) (or 20 to 40 drops of essential oil for 1 ounce of preparation)

The proportions of vegetable butters and oils listed above are a guideline. Any of the ingredients can easily be increased or decreased. Just keep in mind that the more butter there is in the mixture, the thicker it will be at room temperature. The preparation may need to be warmed before application.

The hair care treatment is prepared in the same way as an ointment: melt the butter in a double boiler, then add the oil or infused oil, mix well, and remove from the double boiler. When the mixture starts to cool and thicken, add the essential oil. Pour the mixture into a tinted-glass bottle with a pump lid. Add the essential oil(s) when the mixture is still warm—if it was heated. Finally, shake the bottle so the essential oil(s) are well mixed into the rest of the preparation.

Sample Recipes

Preparation for Damaged Hair

15 g (½ oz.)	Kokum butter
20 ml (⅔ fl. oz.)	Hemp vegetable oil
15 ml (½ fl. oz.)	Castor vegetable oil
15 drops	Atlas Cedar essential oil

Preparation for Preventing Hair Loss

20 ml (⅔ fl. oz.)	Castor vegetable oil
20 ml (⅔ fl. oz.)	Camelina vegetable oil
10 ml (⅓ fl. oz.)	Apricot kernel vegetable oil
20 drops	Altas Cedar essential oil
10 drops	Bay rum essential oil

When stored in pump bottles, hair care preparations are easy to use and they keep well in the refrigerator. If the preparation includes enough vegetable butter to make it solid in the fridge, warm the bottle briefly in hot water before applying the preparation. As it is usually meant for weekly or monthly use and not for every day, it is better to keep whatever may be left over of the preparation in the refrigerator rather than at room temperature.

To use a hair care preparation, simply apply the mixture to dry hair, preferably directly on the scalp (just enough to make it "greasy"). After massaging the scalp a little bit, comb or brush your hair so that the preparation goes all along it. You can then cover your head with a towel and leave the mixture in place for one hour to one night. Afterwards, shampoo your hair as normal.

Alternatively, for scalp and hair treatments, simply add a drop or two of essential oils to a small quantity of shampoo when washing your hair. Or use an emulsion, a cream, or a milk.

Pure hydrosols can also be used in the last rinse after shampooing, or sprayed on the hair every day.

LIP BALMS

Lip balms are made of the same ingredients and are prepared in the same way as ointments. They are simply more solid.

The basic formula for a lip balm is:

- 50% vegetable oil (or infused oil)

- 35% vegetable butter

- 15% beeswax

- A few drops of essential oil (3 to 4 drops of essential oil for 1 ounce of lip balm)

or

- 5% vegetable oil (or infused oil)

- 70% vegetable butter

- 25% beeswax

- A few drops of essential oil (3 to 4 drops of essential oil for one ounce of lip balm)

To prepare a lip balm, melt the beeswax, vegetable oil, and vegetable butter in a double boiler and mix them well. Take the mixture off the double boiler and, when it starts to cool and slightly thicken, add the essential oils. Before adding the essential oil, it is possible to test the consistency of the lip balm by putting a few drops on a glass that has been left in the freezer for a while. This will allow you to make the necessary adjustments to the vegetable oil and butter before adding the essential oil(s) and pouring the preparation into an appropriate container.

Sample Recipes
Example 1 (for five 5 ml/.15 oz. tubes)

9 g (⅓ fl. oz.)	Cocoa butter
5 ml (⅙ fl. oz.)	Cranberry seed vegetable oil
7 ml (.25 fl. oz.)	Calendula infused oil
4 g (.15 oz.)	Beeswax
3 drops	Carrot essential oil

Example 2 (for 5 ml tubes)

17 g (.6 oz.)	Shea butter
2 ml (.07 fl. oz.)	Plantain infused oil
6 g (.21 oz.)	Beeswax
3 drops	Rosewood essential oil

On the market, empty 5 ml (.15 oz.) tubes can be found that are intended for lip balms. Fill the tubes when the preparation is still liquid. Tubes are more hygienic than a little jar from which lip balm is scooped out with a finger. Extra tubes of lip balm keep well in the refrigerator.

CREAMS

A cream is an emulsion of oil and water.

Since a cream still contains a significant amount of veg-etable butter and oil, it is rich and more suitable for dry and normal skin, rather than for oily skin. However, by choosing ingredients in this book that are more easily absorbed by the skin, it is possible to create a cream that is more appropriate for normal to oily skin.

The basic formula for a cream is:

- 30% oil-based ingredients (oils, vegetable butters, and infused oils). These form the oil phase.
- 60% water-based ingredients (hydrosols, purified water, and plant infusions). These form the aqueous phase.
- 10% emulsifier or thickener (wax, gum, etc.)
- A few drops of essential oil:
    - 0.5 to 1% for an ordinary preparation (or 5 to 10 drops of essential oil for 1 ounce of cream)
    - 2 to 4% for a more therapeutic preparation (for acne, couperosis, etc.) (or 20 to 40 drops of essential oil for 1 ounce of cream)
- A few drops of cinnamon, thyme (ct thymol), clove or oregano essential oil can be added—about 0.2% of the total preparation (1 to 2 drops per 1ounce of cream), but not more because these essential oils can irritate the skin. Because of their powerful antibacterial properties, these essential oils extend the shelf life of a cream.

The proportions listed above are only a guideline. The many variations in the natural and physicochemical properties of the ingredients make it very difficult to define an exact formula that applies for all recipes. Many websites and blogs have a wide variety of recipes of varying complexity. These sites can be a good source of information and inspiration for preparing creams.

To prepare the cream, place the vegetable oil, butter, and emulsifier for the oil phase (wax, lecithin, etc.) in a double boiler. Melt the ingredients together gently and mix them well. Prepare the aqueous phase by adding the water-soluble emulsifier (e.g., gum) to the water-based ingredients. Slowly add the aqueous phase to the oil phase by pouring in small amounts and mixing vigorously with a whisk or electric mixer after each addition. When the cream has set, gradually add a little vegetable oil and hydrosol in order to adjust the consistency, if necessary. Finally, take the mixture off the double boiler and add the essential oil, mixing gently. When the mixture is perfectly emulsified, pour the cream into a jar made of tinted glass.

Some recipes recommend mixing the oil phase and the aqueous phase when they are both at 65°C (150°F), and continuing to stir them until the mixture cools off. Others suggest pouring the cold aqueous phase into the oil phase when the latter is lukewarm.

Be careful not to prepare too much of a cream, as it is an emulsion that can separate and is also sensitive to bacterial contamination.

Sample Recipes
Cream for Mixed-Skin Type
8 ml (.26 fl. oz.)   Macadamia nut vegetable oil
7 ml (.25 fl oz)   Hazelnut vegetable oil

5 g (.15 oz.)	Beeswax
30 ml (1 fl. oz.)	Witch hazel hydrosol
2 g (.07 oz.)	Acacia gum
6 drops	Palmarosa essential oil
4 drops	Rosemary ct verbenone essential oil

Cream for Mature Skin

5 g (.15 oz.)	Shea butter
5 ml (.15 fl. oz.)	Argan vegetable oil
10 ml (⅓ fl. oz.)	Wheat germ vegetable oil
3 ml (.1 fl. oz.)	Lecithin (soya)
2 g (.07 oz.)	Xanthan gum
30 ml (1 fl. oz.)	Rose hydrosol
15 drops	Helichrysum essential oil
15 drops	Rock rose essential oil

It may take a while to get the feel for preparing emulsions. The technique is similar to whipping cream or making mayonnaise. It doesn't necessarily work every time. Furthermore, since natural emulsifiers are less effective than synthetic ones, the emulsion may eventually separate—often because of frequent and rapid changes in temperature.

The main difficulty in making creams is to use care not to introduce bacteria. All instruments and containers must be sterilized by boiling them. These homemade creams contain few preservatives, unless they contain essential oils that have effective antibacterial properties. Since creams include aqueous ingredients that are conducive to the development of bacteria and mold, creams must be kept in the refrigerator and used quickly—within weeks of their preparation. For the same reasons, a clean spatula should be used to take cream from the jar.

LOTIONS (OR MILKS)

A skin care lotion is similar in nature to a cream and is prepared in the same way. The only difference lies in the proportion of the aqueous phase, which is greater in a lotion than in a cream, and gives a more fluid consistency.

Since a lotion contains a significant amount of aqueous ingredients (water or aromatic hydrosol), it is usually more suitable for normal to oily skins than creams or ointments.

The basic formula for a lotion is:

- 20% oil-based ingredients (oils, vegetable butters, and infused oils). These form the oil phase.

- 70% water-based ingredients (hydrosols, purified water, and plant infusions). These form the aqueous phase.

- 10% emulsifier or thickener (wax, gum, etc.)

- A few drops of essential oil:

  - 0.5 to 1% for an ordinary preparation (or 5 to 10 drops of essential oil for 1 ounce of lotion)

  - 2 to 4% for a more therapeutic preparation (for acne, couperosis, and so on) (or 20 to 40 drops of essential oil for 1 ounce of preparation)

- A few drops of cinnamon, thyme (ct thymol), clove, or oregano essential oil can be added—about 0.2% of the total preparation (1 to 2 drops for one ounce of lotion), but not more because these essential oils can irritate the skin. Because of their powerful antibacterial properties, these essential oils extend the shelf life of a milk.

A lotion is prepared in the same way as a cream. To obtain a very fluid lotion, it is preferable to use a vegetable oil (as the oil phase) and soya lecithin (as the emulsifier), rather than vegetable butters and beeswax.

Be careful not to prepare too much of a lotion, as it is an emulsion that can separate and is also sensitive to bacterial contamination.

Sample Recipes

Lotion for Irritated Skin

5 ml (.15 fl. oz.)	Avocado vegetable oil
5 ml (.15 fl. oz.)	Lily infused oil
5 g (.15 oz.)	Beeswax
15 ml (½ fl. oz.)	Lemon balm hydrosol
20 ml (⅔ fl. oz.)	Roman chamomile hydrosol
2 g (.07 oz.)	Acacia gum
6 drops	Geranium essential oil
4 drops	Blue tansy essential oil

Lotion for Damaged Skin

4 g (.14 oz.)	Coconut butter
2 ml (.07 fl. oz.)	Sea buckthorn vegetable oil
4 ml (.14 fl. oz.)	Raspberry seed vegetable oil
6 ml (.21fl. oz.)	Avocado vegetable oil
3 ml (.1 fl. oz.)	Lecithin (soya)
2 g (.14 oz.)	Acacia gum
35 ml (1.17 fl. oz.)	Cornflower hydrosol
15 drops	True lavender essential oil
10 drops	Green myrtle essential oil
15 drops	Palmarosa essential oil

A lotion is just as tricky to prepare as a cream and also has the same disadvantages as a cream. On the other hand, since a lotion is more liquid, it is easily stored in a pump bottle, which makes the lotion easier to manipulate and limits its exposure to air, bacteria, and fungus. If the emulsion separates, simply shake the bottle vigorously before each use to recreate the emulsion temporarily.

Keep a small glass or plastic-tinted bottle of lotion on your bathroom counter (away from direct sunlight) for daily use, as long as it contains the quantity needed for one month, but not more. If a larger quantity is made, keep the rest of the preparation in other bottles in the refrigerator.

For people who absolutely want a cream or a lotion but find it too difficult to prepare their own, it is possible to purchase fragrance-free neutral emulsions of a certain quality. They will contain preservatives and emulsifiers; be sure to check the nature and quality of the ingredients. To these emulsions, add a few drops of essential oils as an active ingredient or for the simple pleasure of their aroma.

Important Note

All of these preparations, as well as their ingredients, require a certain minimum care. Essential oils must be stored in tinted-glass bottles away from air and heat. They must be kept in glass rather than plastic because they interact with certain plastics. And the glass must be tinted to protect them from oxidation due to light.

Hydrosols, ointments, and emulsions can be stored in tinted-plastic containers made of PET (polyethylene terephthalate) because of the small amount of aromatic molecules that they contain. Glass is, however, less permeable to bacteria that can contaminate hydrosols and preparations containing aqueous ingredients.

OTHER USES

Masks

Masks must be prepared just before use. They do not keep very well in general. Leave them on your face for ten to twenty minutes (they should be removed immediately if tingling or tightening is experienced).

There are many recipes for masks made of natural products. It is always possible to replace the juice or water with hydrosols and add 2 or 3 drops of an essential oil of your choice.

Here are two recipes for masks that include essential oils, hydrosols, and vegetable oils in their list of ingredients.

Cleaning Mask

15 g (.52 oz.)	Green-, white-, red-, or yellow-powdered clay
10 ml (⅓ fl. oz.)	Hydrosol(s) of your choice (choose one from the ingredients section of this book, based on your skin type)
15 ml (½ fl. oz.)	Vegetable oil of your choice (choose one from the ingredients section of this book, based on your skin type)
4 drops	Essential oil(s) of your choice (choose one from the ingredients section of this book, based on your skin type)

Mix the ingredients and apply to your face.

Regenerative Mask

5 g (.15 oz.)	Brewer's yeast
10 ml (⅓ fl. oz.)	Musk rose oil
5 g (.15 oz.)	Almond butter
5 ml (.15 fl. oz.)	Carrot hydrosol
2 drops	Spike lavender essential oil

Mix the ingredients and apply to your face.

Essential Oils in the Bath

Essential oils do not mix readily into water. You should first dilute the essential oil in a glass of milk (which contains butterfat, a natural solvent for essential oils), and then pour the milk into the bathwater. The essential oil will be dispersed in the water as tiny droplets.

A FEW ADDITIONAL RECIPES

Aromatic Toothpaste

25 ml (⅚ fl. oz.)	Sunflower or sesame vegetable oil
4 ml (.14 fl. oz.)	Plantain or calendula infused oil
15 drops	Tea tree essential oil
5 drops	Clove or laurel essential oil
5 drops	Peppermint or spearmint essential oil

Pour 3 to 5 drops of the mixture onto a toothbrush. This mixture is antiseptic, regenerative for the gums, and refreshing.

Deodorant

25 ml (⅚ fl. oz.)	Geranium hydrosol
20 ml (⅔ fl. oz.)	Roman chamomile hydrosol
3 g (.1 oz.)	Acacia gum
5 drops	Scotch pine essential oil

| 5 drops | Petitgrain bigarade essential oil |
| 5 drops | Palmarosa essential oil |

Dissolve the acacia gum in the hydrosols and pour into a spray bottle. Add the essential oils and shake vigorously. The preparation is ready for use (2 to 3 sprays for each underarm).

Because of the sweet light aromas, as well as their antibacterial properties (palmarosa and Scotch pine) and antiperspirant properties (Scotch pine and petitgrain bigarade), these three essential oils are perfectly suited to this purpose. They slow down perspiration without stopping it completely, and they prevent odors. They are reasonably priced. As an ad might say: With this deodorant you're protected for 24 hours—or more!

Anti-lice Preparation

5 ml (.15 fl. oz.)	Karanja or neem vegetable oil
45 ml (1.5 fl. oz.)	Jojoba vegetable oil
10 drops	Tea tree essential oil
10 drops	Lavandin or true lavender essential oil

Leave this preparation on the hair for one to two hours. Then comb the hair with a fine-toothed comb and shampoo.

As a preventive measure, apply a drop of a mixture of tea tree and lavandin (or true lavender) essential oils (without vegetable oils) to the nape of the neck and the temples. You can also spray a mixture of Atlas Cedar or true lavender (or lavandin) hydrosols on the same spots.

Anti-mosquito Preparation

4 ml (.14 fl. oz.)	Karanja or neem vegetable oil
10 drops	Lemon eucalyptus essential oil
10 drops	Spike lavender essential oil

Lightly moisten your hand and put a few drops of this preparation in the palm. Rub hands together vigorously, and then rub the preparation on the body and face (taking care to avoid your eyes). Repeat the procedure as often as necessary.

In addition to repelling mosquitoes, the essential oils compensate for the rather unpleasant odor of neem oil.

Room Freshener/Deodorizer

50%	Hydrosol(s) of your choice
50%	Odorless alcohol (vodka, for example)
20–30 drops	Essential oil(s) of your choice (per 100 ml or 3 ⅓ fl. oz.)

Mix the alcohol and essential oils in a spray bottle. Add the hydrosol (which makes the preparation somewhat milky), and the preparation is ready for use. This is not as effective as a true diffuser, but it is a good way to recycle any hydrosols that have passed their "best before" date but are still in excellent condition. And, a personal combination of aromas can be created.

Safe Insecticide for Plants

30 ml (1 fl. oz.)	Karanja or neem vegetable oil
4 liters (8.5 pints)	Water
5 ml (.15 fl. oz.)	Liquid soap (to emulsify the oil and water)

The insecticidal and insect-repellent properties of karanja and neem oils are also beneficial for the plants. Spray this mixture on plants that are infested with insects and parasites.

Please note that the use of essential oils is not recommended for infants or babies for cosmetic purpose because, among other concerns, their olfactory system is very sensitive. It is suggested to make specific preparations just for them, without any aromatic ingredients.

Additionally, it would be a good idea to cut by half the proportions of aromatic ingredients in products destined for use on children, compared to those offered in the recipes above for adults.

Soap

Good quality vegetable oils are important ingredients in good quality soap. When making your own cold-process soap, it is a good idea to incorporate the more delicate and more expensive oils in trace amounts in order to limit their degradation by direct contact with pure soda (sodium hydroxide).

Though essential oils are very easy to incorporate in liquid soaps, you might well wonder what happens to their dermocosmetic properties when they are incorporated into solid soaps. Contact with soda that is not yet saponified and exposure to heat and air while the soap is setting and curing undoubtedly affect the aromatic molecules of essential oils.

MEASUREMENTS

Here are a few guidelines on how to measure the ingredients for the recipes in this part of the book.

Measuring Aqueous Substances

Grams and milliliters are interchangeable (1 g = 1 ml = $\frac{1}{30}$ oz.) for aqueous substances. Even if the correspondence is not 100% exact for oily substances, you can still use it because the recipes in this book use such small quantities.

Measuring Spoons

Measuring spoons often have the metric equivalents written on the handle. These are the usual equivalencies:

   1 Tablespoon (Tbsp) = 15 ml = 15 g
   1 teaspoon (tsp) = 5 ml = 5 g

   It is preferable to measure ingredients in grams or ounces using a scale because it is much more precise.

Measuring Essential Oils

Because of the small quantities used, essential oils are usually measured in drops or in milliliters.

   1 ml = 1 g = $\frac{1}{30}$ fl. oz. = 30 to 35 drops

Measuring Solid Ingredients

You must use a scale to measure solid ingredients like vegetable butters and beeswax, since they are hard and cannot be measured with measuring spoons. It is not recommended to melt the approximate amount in a microwave and then use a measuring spoon to get the exact amount needed because the less you manipulate and warm butters, the better. Some ingredients, like beeswax, become very sticky when they are warmed.

EQUIPMENT REQUIRED

Here is a list of the equipment you may need. All of it might not be necessary; it depends on the recipes. All of the utensils can be purchased in kitchen-supply stores.

- An electronic kitchen scale A scale of the required precision (resolution or increments of 1 to 2 grams/0.1 oz.) will cost about $50, which is a good investment since it can be used for cooking as well. Nowadays, many electronic scales can measure in U.S. and metric units.

- A candy thermometer (can be found in kitchen-supply stores)

- 1 or 2 large glass measuring cups with spouts (for heating ingredients in the double boiler, for mixing emulsions, and for pouring preparations into containers, especially lip balm tubes and bottles)

- A double boiler. A small pot and a bowl made of stainless steel, glass, or porcelain can also be used. The pot serves as the lower part of the double boiler in which water is boiled. The bowl serves as the upper part of the double boiler in which the ingredients are melted and mixed.

- A small whisk

- A heat-resistant spatula

- A cheese grater (for beeswax)

- A sieve and coffee-filter holder for filtering any self-prepared infused oils. The preparation of infused oils is explained in Part Two.
- A large pot (large enough to contain enough water to sterilize utensils, bottles, and containers), such as a kitchen pot
- A set of stainless steel measuring spoons
- An electric mixer (reserved for making cosmetic preparations, specifically to prepare large quantities of emulsions)

The following containers can usually be found in stores (including online stores) that sell cosmetic ingredients like butters, oils, and so on:

- Jars and bottles made of tinted glass
- Tubes with inside screws for lip balm

PRACTICAL ADVICE

- When buying ingredients you don't know very well, always buy small quantities, even if they are more expensive that way.
- Begin by buying two or three ingredients only. Over time, continue to buy more until you have a range of ingredients that suit your needs. Then you will only have to stock up on ingredients when you use them up.
- Form a group with other people so you can buy larger quantities of ingredients at a better price and share them.

- For ingredients you don't know well, always ask the sales staff if they have a test container so you can get to know the product a little better. Do not hesitate to ask questions about the products.

- Choose organic ingredients if they are available. Products extracted or processed with chemicals do not meet the criteria for organic certification.

- Begin with the simplest preparations that require the fewest ingredients. This will be easiest. For example: a skin care oil composed of one vegetable oil and one or two essential oils.

- Always make a small quantity when making a preparation for the first time. In this way, you can figure out which preparations you like and want to make again.

- For creams and milks, make the first tests with ingredients that are not too expensive. If the emulsion does not work, it will not have cost a fortune.

- If you are sensitive to odors, reduce the amount of essential oils indicated in the recipes to suit you.

part

T W O

The

Ingredients

This part of the book describes the ingredients. They are grouped by type: vegetable oils, vegetable butters, infused oils, essential oils, and hydrosols. A few emulsifiers are listed at the end.

All the ingredients described are of vegetable origin. As is the rule in botany, and in order to avoid confusion, they are presented under their English name, which is followed by their Latin name, italicized and in parentheses. The Latin name permits an exact identification of the plant in question. This will prevent any potentially harmful misunderstandings that could arise if only the common names were used (which can be different in different countries and regions).

Three

Vegetable Oils (VOs)

VOs are often referred to as "carrier oils," "base oils," or "fixed oils."

These are fats, naturally liquid at room temperature, that are extracted from fruit (nuts, kernels, pits, seeds, pulp). More than two thousand oleaginous plants have been identified around the world.

They have been used since time immemorial as beauty products. Every culture, every region, and every historical period has traditionally used one or the other of these VOs. We are now just beginning to rediscover their beneficial effects and many uses.

The VOs of interest here are extracted in either of two ways: by the first cold-pressed method (the oil is extracted by a mechanical press equipped with a worm screw), or by centrifuge. The first method causes friction and releases heat that must be monitored so that the temperature does not exceed 60°C (140°F). Higher temperatures could degrade the VO.

After extraction, the VO is filtered through a fabric filter first, then through blotting paper. Some VOs are deodorized by a vacuum steam process. Other mechanical filtration processes are also used.

The supercritical CO_2 (carbon dioxide) extraction method is becoming popular, especially for plants that produce a small amount of VO. This technique, which is still expensive, is of high interest because it does not denature the VO in the least.

All VOs that have been extracted by heat or have been processed (neutralizing, bleaching, coloring, chemical de-odorizing, antioxidant treatments, etc.) are to be avoided. Studies show that these techniques contribute to the degrada-tion of antioxidants (tocopherols, tocotrienols, and phenolic acids) that are naturally present in the VOs.

VOs that come from vegetable matter that contain less than 10% fat cannot be extracted by the mechanical-press method. They can only be obtained by use of a solvent—usually hex-ane. (Hexane does not pose a problem only if one can be as-sured that it was used correctly and has totally evaporated from the VO or from all other material that was used in the extrac-tion process.) VOs extracted by the use of solvents cannot be certified organic.

It is preferable to choose a VO that comes from plants raised using organic methods. Heavy metals and the many chemicals, such as pesticides, used in conventional agriculture tend to stick to fats.

A VO keeps its beneficial properties for one to two years, depending on its composition. After this period, many VOs begin to lose their properties gradually. Even when a date appears on the label, it is seldom the production date, which is often impossible to know. A good indication of whether a VO should still be used is whether it has gone rancid. A rancid VO—or any other fat that has gone rancid—gives off a characteristic unpleasant odor. It has oxidized and is, therefore, no longer suitable for use (as a cosmetic or as a food).

VOs have three main enemies: heat, light, and air. The best way to store them is in hermetically sealed glass bottles made of tinted glass. Keeping them in the refrigerator will extend their shelf life significantly (the fact that some oils will congeal or solidify when refrigerated does not affect their properties).

VOs are not simply a medium for active ingredients; they have genuine skin care properties of their own. In general, they are soothing, softening, toning, and restorative for the skin. They protect the skin by reconstructing its protective lipid film, which prevents dehydration while allowing the skin to breathe. This film often suffers from the effects of the environment (cold, dryness, pollution, exposure to sun, over-zealous cleaning). They contain, in amounts specific to each type of VO, vitamins (A, D, E, K), fatty acids (essential fatty acids being also called vitamin F), unsaponifiable matter, and other substances that are indispensable for the elasticity and firmness of the skin. Some VOs contain natural sunscreens. They generally have a sun protection factor (SPF) equal to or less than 5, which is not sufficient for long exposure to full summer sun. Remember that the skin is also nourished from the inside. Eating quality VOs will help to maintain your skin.

Unlike traditional commercial skin products, VOs deeply penetrate the dermis and epidermis. They are also excellent for hair and scalp care. All types of skin and hair can benefit from VOs because each of them has specific characteristics and properties.

People with a history of allergies should be careful in choosing and using VOs, especially nut tree VOs. It should also be noted that VOs rich in squalene, such as olive VO, can contribute to acne.

They can also be used as a makeup remover, for day or night care, for body and hand care, for hair care, as a massage oil, in lip balms and ointments (when mixed with vegetable butters and beeswax), and as milks and creams (in emulsion with hydrosols).

Obviously, those that do not penetrate the skin too quickly are ideal for massages. You can use them individually or mix several of them together. They can be used pure or with essential oils that reinforce the desired effect. They can also be used as the base for preparing infused oils.

The VOs most widely used for skin and hair care are generally quite reasonably priced—around $8–15 per ounce. VOs that are edible can often be found in the food department of health food stores, where they will be much less expensive than a VO of equivalent quality in a cosmetics department or store. This is the case for avocado and hemp VOs. It should be noted that certain VOs, when extracted from roasted nuts or kernels (like macadamias or hazelnuts) are only meant for consumption, not for skin and hair care use.

The descriptions of the VOs have intentionally been separated into two sections. The first section contains the "Classic Vegetable Oils" whose use as skin and hair care products are well known and documented. They are usually very easy to obtain. The second section contains "Exotic Vegetable Oils," which are less well known, but are of great interest for skin and hair care use.

Since rancidity is the main disadvantage of VOs, each VO is given a code that indicates how quickly it tends to go rancid. The codes are only a guideline, since the care with which a VO is packaged and stored will have a considerable influence on how long it stays fresh.

R	goes rancid very slowly
RR	goes rancid slowly
RRR	goes rancid quickly
RRRR	goes rancid very quickly

CLASSIC VEGETABLE OILS

Apricot Kernel (Prunus armeniaca)

The apricot tree is native to central Asia. After being cultivated in China, it spread to Armenia (from which it gets its Latin name). From there, the Romans imported it to the Mediterranean region. The VO is extracted from the kernel of the fruit.

Properties

- regenerating, toning, nourishing, softening
- contains a natural sunscreen

Uses

skin types: oily, mixed, dry, mature, wrinkled, damaged, exposure to the elements (sun, wind, etc.)

hair types: dry, damaged, hair loss

This VO is pale orangey yellow.

Rich in Vitamins A and E.

Very easily absorbed by all skin types, it does not leave a greasy film.

Rancidity: RRR

Argan or Argania (Argania spinosa)

The argan tree grows only in Morocco. The VO, traditionally produced by Berber women, is extracted from the kernel of the fruit.

Properties:

• regenerating, healing, firming, protective, makes the skin and hair more supple, softening

Uses:

skin types: dry, mixed, oily, mature, wrinkled, prone to acne, damaged, chapped, scars, stretch marks (preventive, healing), exposure to the elements (sun, wind, etc.)

hair types: dry, dull

minor burns

This VO is pale and has a very discreet aroma.

The variety of this VO that is used for skin and hair care comes from kernels that have not been roasted. The roasted VO is for consumption only.

Rich in Vitamin E.

Fluid and rapidly absorbed by the skin.

It now has international recognition, which has greatly increased the demand for it, as well as its price. Unfortunately, this newfound fame has given rise to many imitations. It is important to check the source and quality carefully.

Rancidity: RRR

Avocado (Persea gratissima)

The avocado tree is native to central Mexico and is cultivated in all tropical and subtropical regions. The VO is extracted from the pulp of the fruit.

Properties

- regenerating, makes the skin and hair more supple, hydrating, protective, toning

Uses

skin types: dry, fragile (around the eyes and neck), wrinkled, mature, chapped, damaged, exposure to the elements (sun, wind, etc.)

hair types: dry, dull, brittle

eczema

Avocado VO is quite thick and can be somewhat opaque (which is an indication that it has not been refined, is a guarantee of its purity and quality, and does not affect its properties at all). Three different qualities are available in the marketplace:

- bright green, which is made from fresh pulp;
- dark green (almost brown), which is made from dried pulp;
- pale yellow, which has been refined (usually after having been obtained from dried pulp).

Rich in Vitamins A and E.

Very penetrating, easily absorbed by the skin, does not leave a greasy film. Not recommended for oily skins because it is very rich.

Rancidity: R

Borage (Borrago officinalis)

This herb is native to the Middle East. It spread to the Mediterranean and then to all temperate regions. The VO is extracted from the seeds.

Properties

- regenerating, softening, makes the skin, hair, and nails more supple

Uses

skin types: dry, wrinkled, mature, damaged

hair types: dry, damaged

brittle nails

eczema, psoriasis

This VO greatly resembles evening primrose VO. It is yellow and has almost no scent.

Rich in Vitamins A and E.

Absorbed moderately by the skin. It is a good idea to dilute this oil in a more fluid oil.

Higher-than-average price.

Rancidity: RRRR

Castor (Ricinus communis)

This shrub, which is undoubtedly native to northeast Africa and Southeast Asia, is now cultivated in all tropical zones. The VO is extracted from the seeds.

Properties

- softening, healing, nourishing, antipigmentation, antifungal
- strengthens hair, eyelashes, and nails

Uses

skin types: dry, pigmentation spots

hair types: dry, damaged, brittle, hair loss/eyelash loss

brittle nails

fungal infection

Unlike the plant, the VO does not contain any toxic substances.

It is colorless and thick.

Rapidly absorbed by the skin.

Rancidity: R

Evening Primrose (Oenothera biennis)

The evening primrose plant is native to North America and grows in most temperate climates. The VO is extracted from the seeds.

Properties

- regenerating, softening, makes the skin more supple

Uses

skin types: dry, wrinkled, mature, damaged

hair types: dry, damaged

eczema, psoriasis

Evening primrose VO is closely related to borage VO. It is yellow to pale green.

Rich in Vitamin E.

Thick, absorbed moderately by the skin. It is a good idea to dilute this VO in another, more fluid oil.

Priced higher than average.

Rancidity: RRRR

Grape Seed (Vitis vinifera)

This climbing plant is native to Europe and Asia, and is cultivated in all temperate climates. The VO is extracted from the seeds of the fruit.

Properties
• regenerating, astringent

Uses
skin types: oily, mixed, mature, damaged, dilated pores
hair types: brittle, damaged, oily

When extracted by cold pressing and not refined, this VO is green with a pungent aroma, and very expensive.

The odorless and colorless VO that is usually found in stores is extracted by chemical solvents and refined.

Rich in Vitamin E.

Very well absorbed by the skin.

Rancidity: RRRR

Hazelnut (Corylus avellana)

The hazel tree is native to Europe. The VO is extracted from its fruit, the hazelnut. Hazelnuts are also known as filberts.

Properties

• purifying (helps eliminate blackheads), astringent, helps control the production of sebum, nourishing, protective, makes the skin more supple, toning

Uses

skin types: oily, mixed, dry, sensitive, irritated, damaged, dilated pores, blackheads

hair types: dry, oily, damaged

This VO is pale yellow and has a light hazelnut scent.

The VO found in the supermarket or in a health food store is usually made from roasted hazelnuts and has a stronger aroma.

Contains Vitamins A and E.

Fluid and very well absorbed by the skin, does not leave a greasy film.

Rancidity: RRRR

Hemp (Cannabis sativa)

Hemp is native to Central Asia and is cultivated in all temperate climates. The VO is extracted from the seeds.

Properties

• regenerating, softening, firming, healing

Uses

skin types: dry, oily, mixed, mature, wrinkled, prone to acne, damaged

hair types: dry, damaged

eczema

Hemp VO is fluid, rather dark green in color, with a light nutty aroma.

Rich in Vitamin A.

Its chemical composition is close to that of the skin. Penetrates perfectly without leaving a greasy film.

The hemp VO that is available in stores does not contain psychotropic substances.

Rancidity: RRRR

Jojoba (Simmondsia chinensis)

This shrub is native to the semi-desert zones of the southwestern United States. It is also cultivated in South America, the Middle East, and Australia. The VO is extracted from the seeds.

Properties

- very good at controlling the production of sebum, regenerating, calming, protective, softening, anti-inflammatory
- contains a natural sunscreen

Uses

skin types: oily, dry, mixed, prone to acne, sensitive, wrinkled, exposure to the elements (wind, sun, etc.)

hair types: oily, dry

This VO is actually a wax that is liquid at room temperature. It is yellow.

Its composition is very close to that of human sebum. It is very fluid and is absorbed completely by the skin without leaving a greasy film.

Contains Vitamin E.

Rancidity: O (does not go rancid)

Macadamia (Macadamia integrifolia)

The macadamia tree is native to Australia and was introduced to Hawaii and Kenya. It can only be cultivated in a tropical climate. The VO is extracted from the nuts.

Properties

- regenerating, nourishing, protective, softening, healing, soothing, calming

Uses

skin types: dry, oily, mixed, sensitive, irritated, damaged, mature, chapped, scars, stretch marks (healing)

hair types: dry, damaged

This VO is very pale yellow in color and is practically odorless.

It has a thick texture. It is completely absorbed by the skin and leaves it soft and satiny, with no greasy film.

Rancidity: R

Musk Rose or Rosehip Seed
(*Rosa rubiginosa* or *Rosa mosqueta*)

The musk rose resembles the wild rose. It grows throughout the Americas and is widely cultivated in Chile. The VO is extracted from the seeds.

Properties
- highly regenerating and healing, makes the skin more supple, antipigmentation

Uses
skin types: oily, dry, mixed, prone to acne, mature, wrinkled, prone to couperosis, damaged, scars, pigmentation spots, stretch marks (preventive, healing)

hair types: damaged

minor burns and wounds, eczema, psoriasis

This VO comes in various shades of orange and is very fluid.

Rich in Vitamin A, it also contains Vitamin E.

Completely absorbed by the skin, does not leave a greasy film.

More expensive than the average VO.

Rancidity: RRRR

Olive (*Olea europaea*)

The olive tree is native to central Asia. It spread to the Mediterranean and was later introduced to regions of the Americas that have the same climate. There are more than a hundred varieties of olive tree. The VO is extracted from the ripe fruit (and sometimes from fruit that is still green).

Properties

• soothing, nourishing, softening

Uses

skin types: dry, mature, wrinkled, irritated

hair types: dry, damaged

brittle nails

This VO comes in various shades of light green and has an aroma that is more or less pronounced (for skin and hair care, avoid an overly fruity scent).

Contains Vitamins A and E.

Absorbed moderately by the skin.

Rancidity: R

Sesame (Sesamum indicum)

This plant is native to India and grows in tropical and subtropical regions. The VO is extracted from the seeds.

Properties

• regenerating, soothing, softening, somewhat healing, contains a natural sunscreen

Uses

skin types: dry, irritated, exposure to the elements (sun, wind, etc.)

hair types: dry, damaged

Roasted sesame seeds produce an orangey VO with a strong nutty aroma. It is for cooking only.

For skin and hair care, only use the VO obtained from seeds that were not roasted.

It is a very pale yellow and has a slightly acidic scent.

Rich in Vitamin E.

Relatively well absorbed by the skin.

Rancidity: R

Sunflower (Helianthus annuus)

The sunflower is native to North America. The VO is extracted from the seeds.

Properties

• makes the skin and hair more supple, nourishing, softening

Uses

skin types: dry, very dry

hair types: dry

This VO is yellow (more or less pale) and has a fruity aroma similar to that of sunflower seeds.

Contains Vitamin E.

Well absorbed by the skin.

Rancidity: RRR

Sweet Almond (Prunus amygdalus)

The almond tree is native to central Asia and then spread all around the Mediterranean region. The VO is extracted from the kernel of sweet almonds.

Properties

• makes the skin more supple, soothing, toning, softening

Uses

skin types: dry, irritated, chapped   '
minor burns

This VO is a pale yellow color and has a very discreet scent.
Penetrates skin moderately.
Contains Vitamins A and E.
Rancidity: RRR

Wheat Germ (Tricticum vulgare)

This VO is extracted from fresh wheat germ. It is produced
either by soaking the germ in another vegetable oil followed
by cold-press extraction, or directly by using a chemical solvent on the wheat germ.

Properties

• regenerating, soothing, softening, anti-inflammatory, contains a natural sunscreen

Uses

skin types: dry, mature, wrinkled, chapped, damaged, stretch
    marks (healing), exposure to the elements (sun, wind, etc.)
hair types: dry
eczema, psoriasis

When produced directly by solvent, this VO is very dark yel-
    low to brownish red and has a rather strong scent.

Rich in Vitamin E and also contains Vitamin A.

Quite thick, it is absorbed moderately by the skin.

Priced higher than average, especially when produced directly by solvent without presoaking.

Rancidity: RRR

EXOTIC VEGETABLE OILS

Besides the classic VOs, the revival of natural skin and hair care products and foods has put other VOs in the spotlight. New and more exotic VOs are emerging at a great rate. Some had never been extracted before, and others were only produced and used locally. They are becoming more widely available, usually in specialty shops and natural food stores, and on the Internet. As is the case with classic VOs, some are affordable and others are more expensive.

This section lists the new VOs of interest that are currently available—others will continue to appear and become easier to obtain.

Babassu (Orbignya barbosiana)

This palm tree is native to Brazil and also grows in the Caribbean and in Central America. The VO is extracted from the pit of the fruit.

Properties
• nourishing, softening

Uses
skin types: dry, mixed, oily, irritated
hair types: dry, brittle
eczema

This VO solidifies at temperatures below 24°C (75°F). It is practically colorless and odorless.
Rich in Vitamin E.

Very fluid, it is completely absorbed by the skin and does not leave a greasy film.

Rancidity: R

Baobab (Adansonia digitata)

The baobab, which is native to East Africa, has spread over the whole continent and Madagascar. The VO is extracted from the kernel of its fruit.

Properties

• regenerating, softening, nourishing

Uses

skin types: dry, mature, wrinkled, damaged, chapped, stretch marks

hair types: dry

brittle nails

psoriasis, eczema

This VO is yellow (more or less deep) and has a nutty aroma.

Rich in Vitamin E.

Fluid, it is rapidly absorbed by the skin.

More expensive than the average VO.

Rancidity: RR

Camellia (Camellia sinensis)

This shrub, a member of the tea family, is native to Southeast Asia and is widely cultivated in Japan and China. The VO is extracted from the seeds. The oil is also extracted from two other species of camellia: *Camellia oleifera* and *Camellia japonica*.

Properties

- highly softening, regenerating, nourishing, antioxidant strengthening for the hair

Uses

skin types: dry, oily, mixed, mature, wrinkled, irritated, damaged, pigmentation spots

hair types: dry, damaged, dandruff

This VO is yellow. It is the traditional beauty oil of Japanese women.

Very rapidly absorbed by the skin, does not leave a greasy film.

Rancidity: R

Camelina (Camelina sativa)

This herb (usually known as gold-of-pleasure or false flax, also occasionally as wild flax, linseed dodder, German sesame, and Siberian oilseed) is native to the Near East, and has been present in Europe for centuries. The VO is extracted from the seeds.

Properties

- softening, nourishing, protective
- strengthening for the hair

Uses

skin types: dry, sensitive, stretch marks, exposure to the elements (sun, wind, etc.)

hair types: dry, damaged

psoriasis, eczema

This VO is yellow and has a light aroma that is similar to that of linseed oil.

Rich in Vitamin E.

Rapidly absorbed by the skin.

Rancidity: R

Cranberry Seed (Vaccinium macrocarpon)

This shrub is native to North America and belongs to the same family as the blueberry. It grows in the northern United States, in Canada, in Europe, and in northern Asia. The VO is extracted from the seeds of the fruit.

Properties

- regenerating, protective, softening
- strengthening for the hair
- contains a natural sunscreen

Uses

skin types: dry, mature, wrinkled, damaged, exposure to the elements (wind, sun, etc.)

hair types: damaged, dandruff

eczema, psoriasis

This VO has only become available recently. It has not been studied very well, and not all of its skin and hair care properties are well known.

It is yellow-green and has a slightly acidic aroma.

Rich in Vitamin E.

Even though it is rather thick, it is rapidly absorbed by the skin.

More expensive than average.

Rancidity: RR

Karanja (Pongamia glabra)

The karanja is a small tree that is native to Asia. It is found especially in India, but also in many other regions of Asia and in the Pacific as far as Australia. The VO is extracted from the pit of the fruit.

Properties
- regenerating, antibacterial insecticide and insectifuge (with no toxic effects on people and other warm-blooded animals)

Uses
skin types: wrinkled, mature, prone to acne, damaged

hair: parasites (lice)

psoriasis, eczema

This VO is orange to dark brown and has a rather strong aroma that is often considered unpleasant (though less so than the aroma of the VO of neem, with which it shares many characteristics).

Thick, moderately absorbed by the skin.

More expensive than average.

Rancidity: RR

Kukui (Aleurites moluccana)

The candlenut tree is native to Asia and is found especially in Hawaii, Indonesia, and New Caledonia. The VO is extracted from the nuts.

Properties

- regenerating, protective, softening, soothing
- strengthening for the hair

Uses

skin types: dry, oily, mixed, mature, sensitive, irritated, prone to acne, chapped, damaged

hair types: damaged, hair loss

minor burns, psoriasis, eczema

This VO is pale yellow and has a light nutty aroma.

Very easily absorbed by the skin, does not leave a greasy film.

Rancidity: RRRR

Marula (Sclerocarya birrea)

The marula tree is native to southern Africa. The VO is extracted from the kernel of the fruit.

Properties

- regenerating, nourishing, soothing, healing, makes the skin and hair more supple, protective

Uses

skin types: dry, wrinkled, irritated, damaged

hair types: dry, damaged

This VO is pale orangey yellow.

Contains Vitamin E.

Even though it is thick, it is well absorbed by the skin.

More expensive than average.

Rancidity: R

Meadowfoam *(Limnanthes alba)*

This herb is native to the west coast of North America (British Columbia, Oregon, California). The VO is extracted from the seeds. It is said that its name came from the fact that the plant, when in flower, looks like the foam of the ocean.

Properties

- very good at controlling the production of sebum, regenerating, nourishing, softening, soothing, protective

Uses

skin types: dry, mixed, oily, mature, wrinkled, irritated, damaged, exposure to the elements (wind, sun, etc.)

hair types: dry, oily, damaged

This VO was discovered recently and production only began in the 1980s.

Unfortunately, it is often extracted by solvent. It is important to check the production method of any meadowfoam VO used for skin and hair care purposes.

It is reddish yellow and has a light aroma of cucumber peel.

Very fluid, it is absorbed very rapidly by the skin and does not leave a greasy film.

Rancidity: R

Neem (Azadirachta indica)

This tree is native to India and is found in all tropical regions and on the perimeter of the Mediterranean Sea. The VO is extracted from the seeds.

Properties

- excellent at fighting infection (bacterial, viral, fungal), anti-inflammatory, regenerating
- insecticide and insectifuge (with no toxic effects on people and other warm-blooded animals)

Uses

skin types: prone to acne, dry, irritated, damaged

hair types: damaged, dandruff, parasites (lice)

eczema, psoriasis, fungal infection, cold sores (labial herpes)

This VO is greenish brown and solidifies at temperatures below 20°C.

Its spicy aroma, which contains a hint of garlic, is not appreciated by everyone.

Well absorbed by the skin.

Rancidity: R

Nigella or Black Cumin (Nigella sativa)

This plant is native to the Middle East. The VO is extracted from its tiny black seeds.

Properties

- regenerating, healing, softening, fights infection (bacterial, fungal), anti-inflammatory
- strengthening for the hair

Uses

skin types: dry, irritated, prone to acne, mature, damaged

hair types: damaged, hair loss

psoriasis, eczema, fungal infection, minor burns and wounds

This VO is also called the "oil of the pharaohs" because it was held in great esteem and used during their era.

If used pure, it can be irritating for sensitive skin.

Contains Vitamin E and aromatic molecules.

It is dark brown and has a strong aroma reminiscent of fresh wood chips.

Quite thick, it is absorbed by the skin moderately.

Rancidity: RR

Prickly Pear or Cactus Pear (Opuntia ficus indica)

The Indian fig tree is a cactus that is native to Mexico. It is now found in many countries. The VO is extracted from the seeds.

Properties

- highly regenerating, softening, nourishing, protective
- strengthening for the hair

Uses

skin types: mature, wrinkled, damaged, sensitive, oily, dry, mixed

hair types: dry, damaged

This VO has only recently arrived in the marketplace. Complete information about its skin and hair care properties is not yet available.

It should not be confused with the infused oil of the same plant. That one is obtained by soaking the flowers of the prickly pear in another VO, which gives a less expensive and also less active product.

It is greenish yellow and has a light aroma.

Very rich in Vitamin E.

Rapidly absorbed by the skin.

More expensive than average.

Rancidity: R

Raspberry Seed (Rubus idaeus)

Raspberries are native to Europe and Asia. Today they are found in all temperate regions of the world. The VO is extracted from the seeds of the fruit.

Properties

- regenerating, healing, anti-inflammatory, softening
- strengthening for the hair
- contains a natural sunscreen

Uses

skin types: oily, dry, mixed, mature, wrinkled, irritated, prone to acne, damaged, exposure to the elements (wind, sun, etc.)

hair types: damaged, hair loss

eczema, psoriasis

This VO is yellow-green and has an aroma that is reminiscent of linseed oil with a hint of raspberry.

Rich in Vitamin E.

Rapidly absorbed by the skin, it does not leave a greasy film.

More expensive than average.

Rancidity: RR

Rice Bran (Oryza sativa)

Rice is native to Southeast Asia. The VO is extracted from the bran of the grain.

Properties

- highly softening, protective, nourishing, anti-inflammatory, antioxidant

Uses

skin types: dry, mixed, oily, mature, sensitive, irritated

hair types: dry, damaged

Given its small yield, this VO can only be extracted by use of a chemical solvent or by macerating the bran in another VO (followed by cold-press extraction).

When it is raw, its color is orange to brown, and it can be opaque when it contains natural waxes. A new mechanical refining process (that does not involve chemicals) has recently been developed. Unfortunately, most of the VO available on the market has been refined chemically.

Very rich in Vitamin E (tocotrienols).

Easily absorbed by the skin, it does not leave a greasy film. Leaves the skin feeling genuinely soft.

Rancidity: R

Sea Buckthorn (Hippophaë rhamnoides)

This prickly cold-resistant shrub is native to Asia. First, it spread to Europe and later to North America. Now it grows on all three continents. The VO is extracted from the pulp and seeds of the berries.

Properties

- highly regenerating, protective, softening, healing, anti-inflammatory, antibacterial
- strengthening for the hair
- contains a natural sunscreen

Uses

skin types: dry, wrinkled, mature, prone to acne, irritated, damaged, scars, exposure to the elements (sun, wind, etc.)

hair types: dry, hair loss, dandruff

minor burns, eczema

Several types of VO are made from sea buckthorn:

- The VO that comes from the seeds is of the most interest for cosmetic uses. It is orange with a light fruity aroma and goes rancid quickly. It is rich in Vitamin E and contains Vitamin A.

- The VO that comes from the pulp of the fruit is deep orange (it is rich in carotene) and has a strong scent of strawberries. It goes rancid very slowly. It is rich in Vitamin A and contains some Vitamin E.

- The VO made from the pulp and seeds has a color and odor somewhere between the first two types of VO. It is rich in Vitamins A and E. It goes rancid at an average rate.

- The VO made by soaking the fruit of the sea buckthorn in another VO. This is the poorest quality.

Well absorbed by the skin.

It should only be used as 1–5% of the total ingredients in a cosmetic preparation. If it is used in too great a proportion, it will stain the skin (temporarily) and clothing.

Much more expensive than average.

Ranciditiy: depends on the type.

Tamanu (Calophyllum inophyllum)

This tree is native to tropical Asia and is now found throughout Oceania. It is also known as foraha and kamani. The VO is extracted from the kernel of the fruit.

Properties

- highly anti-inflammatory, regenerating, healing, circulatory, fights infection (bacterial, viral), analgesic

Uses

skin types: dry, oily, mixed, irritated, prone to acne, prone to couperosis, mature, wrinkled, chapped, damaged, scars

minor burns, varicose veins, eczema, cold sores (labial herpes—in combination with antiviral essential oils)

This VO is green and has a characteristic aroma that is a little like celery.

Contains Vitamin E.

Rapidly absorbed by the skin, does not leave a greasy film. More expensive than average.

Rancidity: RRR

Watermelon or Kalahari Melon Seed (Citrullus lanatus)

This small wild melon, also known as ootanga and tsamma, is native to southern Africa. The VO is extracted from its seeds.

Properties

- highly antiseborrheic, regenerating, makes the skin more supple

Uses

skin types: oily, mixed, mature, damaged

hair types: oily, damaged

This VO is pale yellow and fluid. It is very well absorbed by the skin and does not leave a greasy film.

Rancidity: RRR

Four

Vegetable Butters (VBs)

VBs are fats with the same general properties as the vegetable oils. The difference between these two types of ingredients is their consistency. VBs are naturally solid at room temperature. They melt at skin temperature. That is why they are used to thicken preparations (milks, creams, ointments, lip balms). They can also be applied to the skin in their pure form (after they have been melted in the palm of the hand).

Unlike vegetable oils, VBs are produced by a process that involves heating the source material (pulp, seeds, or kernels) after it has been ground, in order to extract the fat.

Similar to vegetable oils, some VBs can be extracted by the use of chemical solvents, such as hexane, in order to obtain a higher yield. It is therefore important to determine the production method that was used to obtain a product. (Organic certification of a basic ingredient excludes the possibility that it was extracted by solvent.)

The VBs that are available on the market have often been refined chemically. This allows them to have a longer shelf life, a softer consistency, a lighter color (white), and no odor—features that are desired by consumers who are not well informed.

For VBs, as for all the ingredients presented in this book, if you wish to enjoy their full benefits, it is preferable to choose only those products that have been extracted by mechanical processes, that have been refined or purified only by physical means, and that have not been bleached or deodorized chemically.

The directions for storing VBs are identical to those for vegetable oils: they should be stored away from air, heat, and light. Keeping them in the refrigerator will extend their shelf life.

Because of the popularity of shea butter, you will now see some so-called butters that do not exist in a natural state.

Shea and Golden Shea

These two butters come from two entirely different species of trees. The first tree is the *Butyrospermum parkii*—the source of genuine shea butter. The second tree is the *Pentadesma butyracea*—the butter from the nuts of this tree is also called "pentadesma" or "kpang-nan." Its aroma is less strong and less persistent, its color is deeper (a golden yellow), its consistency at room temperature is firmer (similar to that of cocoa butter), and its texture is soft and powdery. These two butters have very similar properties.

This is the case, for example, for avocado butter and hemp butter. These are vegetable oils that have been hydrogenated (like margarine) or mixed with another hydrogenated fat, which makes them solid at room temperature. What is the true skin and hair care value of these products?

VBs are reasonably priced, around $6 for 100 ml or mg (3.4 fluid ounces). The following pages describe the main VBs that are naturally solid and have a cosmetic interest. As for vegetable oils, the main disadvantage for VBs is that they can turn rancid. The rate at which they tend to go rancid is indicated by codes (which are only a guideline, because the way in which the butters are packaged and stored has an important effect on how long they stay fresh).

R	goes rancid very slowly
RR	goes rancid slowly
RRR	goes rancid quickly
RRRR	goes rancid very quickly

Cocoa (Theobroma cacao)

The cacao tree or cocoa tree is native to Central America and South America. It was introduced to Africa later. The VB is extracted from the seeds.

Properties
• protective, nourishing, softening, makes the skin and hair more supple

Uses
skin types: dry, wrinkled, chapped, exposure to the elements (sun, wind, etc.)

This VB is pale yellow and has a characteristic aroma of chocolate.

Contains Vitamin E.

Very solid at room temperature (breaks in pieces).

Easily absorbed by the skin.

Rancidity: R

Coconut (Cocos nucifera)

The coconut palm is native to the Pacific Islands and grows in all tropical and subtropical zones of the planet. The VB is extracted from the fresh pulp of the nuts. It is considered an oil, even though it is solid at room temperature. It is the basic ingredient of the famous Monoï oil that is widely used in French Polynesia and is popular in Europe.

Properties

• regenerating, protective, soothing, softening, makes the skin and hair more supple

Uses

skin types: dry, sensitive, mature, damaged

hair types: dry, damaged

This VB is white and semi-solid at room temperature. It has an aroma of fresh coconut. The best quality VB is cold pressed, which gives rise to its other names: "coconut oil" and "coco oil."

Contains Vitamin E.

Well absorbed by the skin.

Rancidity: R

Note: This VB should not be confused with copra oil (which is often sold under the name "coconut oil," but is extracted at a high temperature or by a solvent from the dried pulp of the coconut, and has lost its aroma of coconut).

Being edible, Coconut VB can often be found in the food department of a health food store.

Kokum (Garcinia indica)

This tree is native to India and Southeast Asia. The VB is extracted from the kernel of the fruit.

Properties

• highly softening, regenerating, firming, makes the skin and hair more supple

Uses

skin types: dry, sensitive, mature, prone to acne, damaged

hair types: dry, damaged

minor burns

This VB is pale greyish beige. When it is not deodorized, it has a very particular vegetable aroma.

Very firm but melts quickly at skin temperature.

Easily absorbed by the skin, does not leave a greasy film.

Rancidity: R

Mango (Mangifera indica)

The mango tree is native to southern Asia and spread to all tropical regions of the globe. The VB is extracted from the pit of the fruit.

Properties

- makes the skin and hair more supple, nourishing, healing, softening
- contains a natural sunscreen

Uses

skin types: dry, mature

exposure to the elements (wind, sun, etc.)

hair types: dry, damaged

The color of this VB is very similar to that of cocoa butter (as is its composition). Its texture is similar to that of shea butter.

It has a light vegetable aroma.

Easily absorbed by the skin, it does not leave a greasy sensation.

This VB is often extracted by solvent and refined.

Rancidity: R

Sal (Shorea robusta)
Illipe (Shorea stenoptera)

These two trees are native to Asia. The VBs are extracted from the pit of their fruit.

Properties

- nourishing, softening, protective, makes skin and the hair more supple

Uses

skin types: dry, mature, exposure to the elements (wind, sun, etc.)

hair types: dry and damaged hair

The properties and appearance of the VBs are very close to those of cocoa butter, which they sometimes replace in skin and hair care preparations. Sal BV is odorless and does not leave a greasy film.

Rancidity: R

Shea (Butyrospermum parkii)

This tree is native to Sahelian Africa. The VB is extracted from the kernel of its nuts.

Properties

- regenerating, nourishing, softening, makes the skin and hair more supple, healing, anti-inflammatory, protective
- strengthening for the hair
- contains a natural sunscreen

Uses

skin types: dry, wrinkled, irritated, chapped, damaged, scars, stretch marks (preventive), exposure to the elements (sun, wind, etc.)

hair types: dry, damaged

eczema, psoriasis, minor burns and wounds

This VB is a compact paste with a characteristic fruity aroma.

The VB that is beige and silky is considered to be of the best quality. The VB that is pale grey and granular is of inferior quality.

Contains Vitamins A and E.

Absorbed moderately by the skin.

Because of its consistency, this VB must be melted (in the palm of the hand for small quantities, in a double boiler for larger quantities) if using it in its pure form. It must be completely liquid before it is applied and can then be massaged in gently so that it penetrates (the excess can be wiped off with a cloth).

Rancidity: RR

Note

It has been noticed that, if this VB is used to massage the arms and legs before physical exercise, the muscles are in better shape, are more supple, and recover more quickly from the effort.

Five

Infused Oils (IOs)

Also known as "oily macerates," "lipidic extracts," and "maceration oils," IOs are vegetable oils enriched naturally with plant extracts. They have been known, prepared, and used since antiquity and even before.

They are obtained by macerating (a fancy way of saying soaking) plants or parts of plants (flowers, leaves, or roots, depending on the plant chosen) that may be fresh (but not wet) or dried, depending on preference or on the plant, in a vegetable oil. This technique allows extracting the active ingredients that are beneficial to the skin, as well as taking advantage of the desirable effects of the oil used for soaking.

IOs are rarely used pure in skin and hair care products. To make cosmetic preparations, they are usually mixed, in a proportion of up to 50%, with other oils and vegetable butters.

They are very easy to make yourself:

- Put a handful of plants into a glass jar without packing them down. About 100 grams (3.5 oz.) of dried plants is needed for a liter (33.8 fl. oz.) of vegetable oil.

- Cover the plants completely with vegetable oil or a mixture of vegetable oils (chosen for the effect you are seeking or the desired quantity of IO).

- Close the jar and allow the mixture to soak in a sunlit location for one to three weeks, depending on the plant. Stir the contents of the jar every day.

- When the soaking period is complete, filter the mixture. This is done in two steps: first, filter it through a sieve; and second, filter it through a coffee filter or a fine cloth in order to remove all impurities.

- Pour the filtered oil into a bottle of tinted glass.

- Take care not to include the sediment from the bottom of the container when fresh plants are used. The sediment includes aqueous substances that could cause fermentation.

- It is possible to repeat the soaking process with the IO just made in order to obtain a higher concentration of active ingredients.

Follow the same directions for storage as were given for vegetable oils. The rancidity rating of the vegetable oil used for soaking applies to the IO.

The cost of an IO depends mostly on the vegetable oil used to make it. Because they are not too expensive, olive oil, sesame oil, and sunflower oil are good for preparing IOs.

Calendula (Calendula officinalis)

This very common plant, more widely known as the marigold, is native to the Mediterranean basin. It can be grown in a pot as well as in earth. The IO is prepared from the flowers.

Properties

• soothing, regenerating, antiseptic, healing, anti-inflammatory, circulatory, softening

Uses

skin types: dry, sensitive, irritated, chapped, mature, wrinkled, prone to acne, damaged, scars, prone to couperosis

hair types: dry, damaged

minor burns, cracks, and wounds, eczema, fungal infection, insect bites, varicose veins

The IO is orangey-yellow in color.

Soaking time is 14 to 21 days.

Carrot (Daucus carota var. sativa)

This vegetable is native to the Middle East. The IO is prepared from the root of cultivated carrots.

Properties

• protects against the ravages of the sun, regenerating, softening, makes the skin more supple

Uses

skin types: sensitive to the sun (apply before and after exposure), prone to acne, chapped

eczema, psoriasis, sun allergies

This IO is bright orange. It should be used in small quantities
(diluted to 5 to 10% of the preparation) in order to avoid
staining the skin (temporarily) and clothing.

Soaking time is 21 days.

Comfrey (Symphytum officinale)

Comfrey is a common plant that is native to Europe and temperate regions of Asia. It is easy to find in the North American countryside. The IO is prepared from the large leaves of
the plant.

Properties

• highly healing and regenerating, antiseptic, soothing, antipigmentation

Uses

skin types: prone to acne, irritated, damaged, chapped, pigmentation spots, scars

minor burns and wounds, psoriasis, eczema

Some studies have shown that comfrey can be harmful for the
liver, though the doses studied were controversial. Since
then, the sale of preparations for internal use is forbidden,
in particular in Canada and the United States. It is not recommended to apply comfrey to large open wounds.

Soaking time is 21 days.

Daisy (Bellis perennis)

The daisy is native to Europe, where it is very common. The
IO is prepared from the flowers.

Properties
- firming and toning for the bust

Uses
lack of firmness of the breasts
Soaking time is 21 days.

English Plantain (Plantago lanceolata) or Greater Plantain (Plantago major)

These two herbs are native to Europe and temperate regions of Asia, and are very common. They are found in almost all uncultivated fields and in the city as well as the countryside. The two plants are the same species so they can be used in the same way. The IO is prepared from the leaves.

Properties
- healing, anti-inflammatory, antiseptic, soothing

Uses
skin types: prone to acne, damaged, irritated, sensitive
minor burns and wounds, insect bites, eczema, psoriasis

This IO is green and has a grassy scent.
Soaking time is 21 days.

Lily—White (Lilium candidum)

The white lily is native to Asia. The IO is prepared from the flowers.

Properties

- regenerating, soothing, softening, clarifying, healing, anti-pigmentation

Uses

skin types: mature, wrinkled, irritated, prone to couperosis, pigmentation spots, sallow complexion

This IO has a delicate lily aroma.

Soaking time is 7 to 10 days.

Six

Essential Oils (EOs)

EOs are the volatile aromatic components of plants that have a scent. They can be found in a specific part of the plant (flower, leaf, root, bark, sap, etc.) or in the entire plant. From a biochemical point of view, they are fatty substances of lipidic nature. But, unlike vegetable oils, they are volatile and, therefore, evaporate completely in air. Before they are distilled, they are called aromatic essences rather than essential oils. Though they are chemically different from fats, they are lipophilic and soluble in oily substances, but not in aqueous substances (like vegetable oils, they float on water and do not mix with it). EOs are composed of various aromatic molecules that are present in proportions specific to each EO. They make excellent active ingredients for skin and hair care products because they have properties of high interest.

EOs can be extracted in several ways:

- In most cases, they are steam distilled, in a still. To obtain a high-quality product, the operation must be performed at low pressure, at a low temperature, and over a period of time sufficient to extract all the aromatic components of the plant (they are not all liberated at the same time in the distillation process). Since the process is well known and time-honored, the properties of the EOs produced in this way are well documented.

- For citrus fruits, the oil is expressed mechanically, or cold-pressed from the peels. It is called an essence.

- Extraction by supercritical CO_2 (carbon dioxide under high pressure) is a relatively recent method. It produces a high-quality aromatic extract that is identical to the aromatic substance originally contained in the plant (because the process does not involve heat or chemical transformation) and contains no trace of solvents (CO_2 is inert and completely evaporates at the end of the process). This process results in a more complete substance than steam distillation (which causes the loss or modification of certain aromatic molecules). Thus, the "EOs extracted by supercritical CO_2" (or "aromatic oils extracted by supercritical CO_2," as world-renowned specialist and researcher Pierre Franchomme recommends calling them) have a chemical composition different from the EOs produced by the traditional steam-distillation method, and therefore, they also have different properties. Many aromatic products produced by CO_2 extraction have not been well studied and documented yet. CO_2 extraction is still complex and expensive, but it is becoming more common. Those products are mostly marketed under the name of "CO_2 extracts," or, improperly, "CO_2 essential oils."

- The enfleurage method consists of placing the plant matter that contains the aroma in a layer of natural fat (the traditional method) or synthetic fat (the more modern method) for a period of time long enough to capture the aromatic substances. The product obtained in this way is called either a "concrete" (a substance containing pigment and wax, as well as about 50% aromatic essence) or an "absolute" (a liquid obtained by treating the concrete with a solvent in order to extract the aromatic substance). This technique is used for aromatic plants that cannot be distilled because they are so fragile (most often for flowers like jasmine, for example). Because of the trace amounts of solvent that may be found in the final product, concretes and absolutes are only used in the perfume industry. They are not appropriate for skin and hair care or therapeutic uses.

- Extraction directly by solvents is very common in the perfume industry. The concretes and absolutes obtained in this way are obviously to be avoided because of the residues of chemical solvents that they may contain.

The heat required for steam distillation causes the modification of certain aromatic molecules. For example, chamazulene (which is dark blue) is found in the EO of German chamomile or yarrow, though it is almost not present in the fresh plant.

The revival of aromatherapy has raised the economic interest in EOs, opening the door to a number of by-products. Here is some advice on how to ensure that you are buying a quality product:

- It is important to check the source of the plant. Preferably, it was wild or cultivated in a "clean" way; if possible, organic. If it was cultivated industrially, it will contain residues of fertilizers, pesticides, and other chemical products used during cultivation and harvest. These residues will be concentrated by the process of distillation.

- The presence of the full name of the plant, in English and Latin, allows you to ensure the botanical origin. According to the region, the country, or the continent, the plants do not always have the same common name. For example, North American cedar trees belong to different botanical families (*thuja, juniperus*, etc.) than the Atlas Cedar tree (*Cedrus atlantica*). The EOs extracted from North American cedars have different properties (and are sometimes toxic) from those of the Atlas Cedar. Similarly, common sage (*Salvia officinalis*) does not have the same biochemical composition nor the same properties as clary sage (*Salvia sclarea*).

- Mention of the country of origin of a distilled plant is also an indication of the rigor and seriousness of the distributors in their choice of products. This shows that they are transparent about their sources and concerned about traceability, and that they wish to guarantee the quality of their products. Certain EOs have vintages, like wines.

- The biochemical composition of certain plants can vary enormously depending on the land, the amount of sunshine, the climatic conditions, and the altitude. This is the case for rosemary, for example. For these plants, it is important to choose an EO whose components are clearly marked and were identified by rigorous chemical analysis. To this end, the notion of chemotype has been developed. You will see the abbreviation "ct" (for chemotype) followed by the name of the molecule that is particular to the EO in question. For example: rosemary ct verbenone (*Rosmarinus officinalis* ct verbenoniferum), rosemary ct cineole (*Rosmarinus officinalis* ct cineoliferum), and rosemary ct camphor (*Rosmarinus officinalis* ct camphoriferum).

- The part of the plant that was distilled should also be mentioned. For example, the EO made from the leaves of the sour orange tree does not have the same properties as the EO made from its flowers or the essence made from the zest of the fruit (and does not have the same price).

The supercritical CO_2 extraction process makes it possible to extract all the lipophilic substances from an aromatic plant. Depending on the pressure and temperature used, different extracts are obtained:

- Total extracts, which include non-volatile lipid substances (fats, waxes, resins, pigments, etc.). The consistency of the product may be more or less thick.

- Selective extracts, which only include the volatile aromatic molecules of the plant. This produces a liquid aromatic essence whose aroma and composition are identical to that of the plant from which it was obtained. It is not recommended to use these extracts in a diffuser: they contain some molecules that are harmful to the lungs.

This process can also be used to extract non-aromatic lipidic substances such as vegetable oils.

An EO may contain more than 10,000 distinct biochemical components (all of which may not have been identified yet). For example, true lavender contains more than a thousand components. It is the presence of certain of these components individually—and more important, in combination—that determines the specific properties of an EO.

EOs cross the skin barrier and penetrate the skin deeply, which makes them of interest for skin care purposes. Then they enter the blood and circulate through the body. Since the amounts used in skin care products are minimal, the impact on the body is small. Nonetheless, people with health issues and pregnant or nursing women should use EOs very carefully and in very small quantities.

EOs should be stored away from air, light, and temperature variations. For this reason, they should be kept in bottles made of tinted glass (brown, blue, or green) with tight-fitting lids. Under these conditions, many EOs can be stored for many years without any changes.

The first signs of a primitive still were found in ancient Persian documents dating from 3500 B.C. Other documents dating from 300 B.C. show that the Greeks and Egyptians carried out a type of distillation. It was Avicenna, the famous Arab philosopher and doctor, who, at the end of the tenth century, perfected the steam distillation process that is still used today. The crusaders introduced the process to Europe in the twelfth century.

The use of EOs in skin and hair care products requires the respect of these simple rules:

- Certain EOs should not be used, especially those that increase photosensitivity (the essences made from citrus peel and the EO of angelica) and those that are irritating to the skin (the EOs of cinnamon bark and cloves, among others).

- It is strongly recommended that people suffering from allergies should test for a reaction by applying a drop of the EO on the inside of the arm before using the EO.

- People with epilepsy should also avoid certain EOs that contain neurotoxic aromatic molecules.

- Avoid all contact with the eyes. (If it happens, rinse the eyes thoroughly with water and then with a vegetable oil.)

- The general rules to follow are: keep EOs out of the reach of children; apply a vegetable oil if there is an undesirable reaction (vegetable oils dilute EOs, which are soluble in fatty substances); pregnant and nursing women should verify that a particular EO is not harmful for them.

- EOS should not be used on infants and babies, and used with caution on young children.

Generally speaking, since skin and hair care products contain such small amounts of EOs, people who have no particular sensitivities or health issues should follow the general precautions explained above.

However, it is essential to pay attention to any contraindications for therapeutic use of each EO, when larger doses are involved.

The main EOs that are of interest in skin and hair care products are those whose properties are antiviral, antibacterial, antifungal, healing, regenerating, anti-wrinkle (they slow the development of wrinkles), astringent, anti-inflammatory, circulatory, regulatory of sebum production or antiseborrheic, insectifuge, and antipigmentation. Some EOs stimulate hair growth and fight dandruff.

Eczema

You are strongly advised against using cortisone medication at the same time as any of the preparations using natural ingredients described in this book.

Mixing the two types of product could provoke the opposite of the desired effect and could aggravate the symptoms. Before starting to use natural ingredients, you must have stopped using products that contain cortisone for several weeks.

In skin and hair care products, EOs should be diluted in a vegetable oil or butter (in a proportion of about 0.5 to 1% for an ordinary preparation, and from 2 to 4% for a "therapeutic" effect—for acne, couperosis, and so on). Remember that EOs are soluble in fats and alcohol, but not in water. They can also be integrated, in the same proportions, into ready-made products, such as milks, creams, ointments, oils, and shampoo. For very localized skin problems, such as acne or cold sores, they can be applied to the spot undiluted, using a cotton swab.

They can be used one at a time, or several can be mixed in the same preparation. Often, two or three complementary EOs can be combined. In this way, you can reinforce a desired effect, work on several desired effects at once, or create a personalized aroma. Do not mix too many EOs together in a single preparation: this would result in many different aromatic molecules and would make it difficult to predict how they would interact.

To obtain approximately one kilogram (2.2 lbs) of EO, the following quantity of the fresh plant is required:

   7 kg (15.4 lbs) of clove buds
   20 kg (44 lbs) of lavandin
   100 kg (220 lbs) of true lavender
   800 kg (1,760 lbs) of geranium leaves
   1,000 kg (1.1 ton) of helichrysum
   more than 4,000 kg (4.4 tons) of roses

In general, the small quantities in which EOs are used in skin and hair care products make them quite affordable. However, certain EOs are quite expensive. The EO descriptions in the following pages include the price range for 15 ml (½ fl. oz.). This range is only a guideline because prices are subject to variations that depend on the annual harvest and, for imported EOs, on exchange rates.

$: less than $10 for 15 ml (½ fl. oz.)
$$: from $10 to $20 for 15 ml (½ fl. oz.)
$$$: from $20 to $40 for 15 ml (½ fl. oz.)
$$$$: from $40 to $100 for 15 ml (½ fl. oz.)
$$$$$: more than $100 for 15 ml (½ fl. oz.)

Bay Rum or West Indian Bay (Pimenta racemosa)

This tree is native to the Caribbean and Central America. It took hold later in various tropical regions of Asia, Africa, and the Pacific. The EO is extracted from the leaves.

Properties

• very good at controlling dandruff and strengthening the hair, antibacterial

Uses

hair types: oily, damaged, dull, dandruff, hair loss

This EO is pale yellow and has a spicy aroma.

It is irritating for the skin and should be used in very small quantities—in the order of 0.5% of the total ingredients of a hair preparation.

Should be avoided during pregnancy.

Price: $$

Benzoin/Siam (Styrax tonkinensis)

This shrub is native to Southeast Asia, and in particular, to Laos. A fragrant resin is extracted by making incisions in the trunk. The resin is distilled to obtain the EO. The resin can also be dissolved in alcohol to obtain a tincture or an absolute (after the alcohol has evaporated).

Properties

• antibacterial, antifungal, regenerating, healing, circulatory, anti-inflammatory

Uses

skin types: dry, chapped, irritated, mature, wrinkled, prone to couperosis, prone to acne

minor wounds, fungal infection

The Siam bezoin (*Styrax tonkinensis*) has an aroma of vanilla more than Sumatra benzoin (*Styrax benzoe* or *benzoin*), whose aroma is more spicy. The two varieties seem to have the same dermocosmetic properties.

The EO can provoke an allergic-type sensitivity, especially if it is applied pure.

Some absolutes and tinctures obtained by the use of chemical solvents should be avoided.

Price: $

Black Spruce (Picea mariana)

This resinous tree is native to Canada. The EO is extracted from the needles.

Properties
- firming and toning for the breasts

Uses

lack of firmness of the breasts

The effect ends if one stops use for a few weeks.

Price: $

Blue Tansy (Tanacetum annuum)

The blue tansy is sometimes called Moroccan blue chamomile, from the country where it grows. The EO is extracted from the flowers.

Properties
- anti-inflammatory, calming, analgesic, anti-allergic

Uses

skin types: irritated, prone to couperosis

eczema, skin allergies, insect bites

This EO is well tolerated by the skin. Its dark blue color (which is due to chamazulene) does not affect cosmetic preparations because of the small quantity of EO used.

Has a fruity, flowery aroma.

It should not be used by people with hormone-dependent cancer.

Note: it should not be confused with the wild tansy (*Tanacetum vulgare*), nor with the Moroccan chamomile (*Ormenis mixta*).

Price: $$$

Carrot (Daucus carota)

The carrot is native to the Middle East and grows wild in uncultivated fields, on riverbanks, and by the roadside. The EO can be obtained from the wild and cultivated varieties of carrot. It is extracted from the seeds.

Properties
- regenerating, firming, healing

Uses

skin types: prone to couperosis, prone to acne, mature, wrinkled, dry, damaged, pigmentation spots (in combination with celery)

eczema

This EO has a sweet smell that is reminiscent of carrots.

Price: $$

Cedar—Atlas (Cedrus atlantica), Cedar—Himalayan (Cedrus deodora)

The Atlas Cedar is native to North Africa. The Himalayan Cedar, as its name indicates, comes from the western Himalayas. The composition of the EOs produced from both species is almost identical. They are extracted from the wood of the tree.

Properties

- healing, antibacterial, dissolves grease, astringent, antiseborrheic, circulatory, insectifuge
- good at controlling dandruff, strengthening the hair

Uses

skin types: oily, prone to acne, prone to couperosis

circles under the eyes

hair types: oily, damaged, dandruff, hair loss

parasites (lice)

cellulite, varicose veins, eczema, psoriasis

This EO has a woody aroma. It is not recommended for pregnant or nursing women, and people with epilepsy.

Note: Not to be confused with the various species of North American cedars (*Thuja, Juniperus, etc.*).

Price: $

Cedar—Eastern Red or Virginian (Juniperus virginiana)

This shrub grows on the East Coast of the United States, where it is usually called red cedar, red juniper, or Virginian Cedar. The EO is extracted from the wood.

Properties

- highly circulatory, astringent, anti-inflammatory, antiseborrheic

Uses

skin types: oily, prone to acne, prone to couperosis, dilated pores

circles under the eyes

hair types: oily

varicose veins

This EO has a thick consistency and a strong, woody aroma.

The EO of juniper berries and branches *(Juniperus communis)* has the same cosmetic properties.

It is not recommended for pregnant and nursing women.

Price: $

Celery (Apium graveolens)

Celery is native to Europe and Asia. The EO is extracted from the cultivated seeds.

Properties

• excellent antipigmentation properties

Uses

pigmentation spots

This EO should not be confused with the EO that is distilled from the whole plant, which causes photosensitivity.

Price: $$

Chamomile – German (Matricaria recutita)

German chamomile, which is native to Europe and western Asia, is also known as blue chamomile. It grows wild by the roadside and in fields. It is also grown in gardens. The EO is extracted from the flowers, which look like small daisies.

Properties

• highly anti-inflammatory, healing, anti-allergic

Uses

skin types: sensitive, irritated, prone to acne, prone to couperosis

eczema, psoriasis, minor burns, skin allergies

This EO is dark blue in color (due to the presence of chamazulene). It is well tolerated by the skin. The color does not have an impact on skin and hair care product preparations because of the small percentage of EO present.

Price: $$$$

Chamomile–Roman (Chamaemelum nobile or Anthemis nobilis)

Roman chamomile, also known as English chamomile, is native to Western Europe and North Africa. It is fond of dry fields and cultivated land. The EO is extracted from its white flowers.

Properties

• analgesic, highly anti-inflammatory

Uses

skin types: prone to couperosis, irritated, sensitive, prone to acne

allergies, eczema, psoriasis, minor burns

This EO is pale green and has a grassy aroma with fruit hints.
Price: $$$$

Clary Sage (Salvia sclarea)

Clary sage, a large plant native to southern Europe and the Middle East, loves dry, sunny terrain. It is cultivated mainly in France, Russia, and North Africa. The EO is extracted from its flowers and/or leaves.

Properties

- regenerating, astringent, antiseborrheic, antiperspirant, anti-inflammatory
- strengthening for the hair

Uses

skin types: prone to acne, oily, wrinkled, mature

hair types: dandruff, hair loss

excessive perspiration

This EO has the advantage of not having the neurotoxic properties of common sage (*Salvia officinalis*). It should not be used by people with hormone-dependent cancer.

Price: $$

Cypress (Cupressus sempervirens)

This tree is native to Asia and is found all around the Mediterranean. The EO is extracted from the young branches.

Properties

- highly circulatory, astringent, deodorizing and antiperspirant, antibacterial, antiseborrheic

Uses

skin types: prone to couperosis, oily

circles under the eyes

hair types: oily

varicose veins, excessive perspiration

This EO has a resiny odor. It should be avoided by people with hormone-dependent cancer and by pregnant and nursing women.

Price: $$

Geranium or Rose Geranium (Pelargonium x asperum)

The geranium, which is native to South Africa, is now cultivated around the world. The EO is extracted from the leaves.

Properties

- fights infection (bacterial, fungal), coagulant, anti-inflammatory, toning, astringent, healing, antiperspirant, insectifuge

Uses

skin types: oily, dry, mixed, prone to acne, wrinkled, mature, irritated, damaged, dilated pores, stretch marks (preventive)

hair types: dandruff

parasites (lice)

eczema, fungal infection, minor wounds and cuts, excessive perspiration

This EO is very effective at controlling acne. It can be applied directly and undiluted for this purpose, without causing a burning sensation.

It has a strong, flowery aroma that is reminiscent of roses. (In fact, it is sometimes used to dilute the EO of rose.)

Its composition varies greatly depending on where it was cultivated. The EO of plants cultivated on l'Île de la Réunion (cv Bourbon) and in North Africa (cv Egypt) is of the most interest and is the most sought-after. The composition and properties of the EO from China (cv China) and from Russia (cv Russia) are different.

(Cv means "cultivar," and designates a plant that has been deliberately selected for its specificity; in this case, its particular aromatic molecules.)

It should be used with caution by pregnant women.

Price: $$

Green Myrtle (Myrtus communis ct cineole)

This shrub is native to the Mediterranean basin. The EO is extracted from the leaves.

Properties

• highly toning for the skin, astringent, controls the production of sebum, fights infection (viral, bacterial), circulatory

Uses

skin types: oily, dry, mixed, prone to acne, irritated, prone to couperosis, wrinkled, mature, damaged, dilated pores, stretch marks (preventive and healing)

hair types: oily, dry

parasites (lice)

varicose veins, cold sores (labial herpes)

The composition of the EO of myrtle varies depending on its source. It is the "green" EO (which contains a lot of cineole), which usually comes from the northern Mediterranean, mainly Corsica, that is of interest here. The EO that comes from North African myrtle is mostly the "red" type; it has a different composition.

It is well tolerated by the skin.

Price: $$$

Helichrysum (Helichrysum italicum)

This plant is part of the everlasting family and is native to the Mediterranean basin. In particular, it is found in Corsica and Sardinia (the most sought-after quality) where it grows wild, as well as the Balkan region (Italy, Bosnia, and so on). The EO is extracted from the flowers.

Properties

- highly regenerating and healing, circulatory, astringent, anti-inflammatory
- anticoagulant
- fights infection (viral, bacterial)

Uses

skin types: prone to couperosis, mature, wrinkled, prone to acne, damaged, scars, dilated pores, stretch marks (preventive and healing)

circles under the eyes

cellulite, varicose veins, cold sores (labial herpes), bruises, eczema

This EO, which has a particular flowery aroma, should be avoided by pregnant women and people with epilepsy.

The great demand for this EO worldwide has led to its rarity and, since 2007, to its cultivation, especially in Corsica.

Price: $$$$

Lavender—Spike (Lavandula latifolia spica)

Like other lavenders, spike lavender is native to the scrubland of the Mediterranean perimeter. The EO is extracted from the flowering tops.

Properties

• fights infection (fungal, viral, bacterial), highly antitoxic, analgesic, healing, regenerating

Uses

skin types: oily, prone to acne, damaged, chapped, stretch marks (preventive)

fungal infection, minor burns and wounds, insect bites and stings (bee, mosquito, spider, jellyfish, etc.), eczema, psoriasis, cold sores (labial herpes)

It is not recommended during the first trimester of pregnancy.

There are several varieties of lavender, each with its own composition and properties. Be careful not to confuse them.

Price: $$

Lavender—True (*Lavandula angustifolia* or *L. officinalis* or *L. vera*)

Like other lavenders, true lavender is native to the scrubland of the Mediterranean perimeter. The EO is extracted from the flowering tops.

Properties

- healing, regenerating, analgesic, anti-inflammatory, antibacterial, astringent, insectifuge

Uses

skin types: oily, prone to acne, prone to couperosis, irritated, damaged, dilated pores, scars, stretch marks (healing)

eczema, psoriasis, minor burns and wounds, insect bites, parasites (lice)

There are several varieties of lavender, each with its own composition and properties. Be careful not to confuse them.

This EO should not be used on very dry skin.

Unfortunately, a tiny insect, the leafhopper, is ravaging the lavender and lavandin plants (both wild and cultivated) of southern France. The insect transmits phytobacteria to the plant, which causes the plant to wither very quickly.

Price: $$

Myrrh (*Commiphora myrrha* or *C. molmol*)

The myrrh or balsam tree is native to East Africa. The EO is extracted from the resin.

Properties

- hydrating, regenerating, healing, anti-inflammatory, fights infection

Uses

skin types: dry, mature, wrinkled, irritated, prone to acne, prone to couperosis

eczema, infection, minor burns and wounds

This amber-colored EO is thick and sticky. It has a characteristic resiny, woody aroma.

Price: $$

Neroli (Citrus aurantium var. amara)

The bigarade orange tree, also known as the bitter or sour orange tree, is native to southern China. It was later introduced to the Mediterranean basin and is now cultivated in all tropical and subtropical zones of the planet. The EO is extracted from the flowers (also known as Neroli or orange blossoms).

Properties

- regenerating, calming, circulatory, healing

Uses

skin types: mature, wrinkled, oily, prone to couperosis, irritated, sensitive

This EO is highly prized in the perfume industry because of its delicate aroma.

Since the EO is very expensive, it is also of interest to use the hydrosol, which is much less expensive.

These days in stores, one can find a mixture composed of 10% neroli EO and 90% vegetable oil, which makes it much more affordable.

Price: $$$$$

Palmarosa (Cymbopogon martinii)

This herb is native to India (it is also known as East Indian geranium), where it grows wild. It is also cultivated there, as well as in other countries, including in Africa and South America. The EO is extracted from the entire plant.

Properties

• excellent at fighting infection (bacterial, viral, fungal), regenerating, controls the production of sebum, healing, astringent, hydrating

Uses

skin types: oily, dry, mixed, prone to acne, wrinkled, mature, irritated, chapped, damaged, dilated pores

hair types: oily, dry, dandruff

fungal infections, eczema, minor wounds, cold sores (labial herpes)

This EO has a light flowery aroma that is a little reminiscent of rose and geranium, with a hint of lemon. It is sometimes used to dilute rose EO.

Because of its high geraniol content, it may cause allergic reactions.

It should not be used by pregnant women.

Price: $

Patchouli (Pogostemon cablin)

This shrub is native to Asia and is cultivated mainly in Indonesia. The EO is extracted from the leaves.

Properties

• regenerating, circulatory, anti-inflammatory, astringent

Uses

skin types: dry, irritated, prone to acne, prone to couperosis, mature, wrinkled, damaged, dilated pores

hair types: dandruff

skin allergies, eczema, varicose veins

A symbol of the hippie period, the persistent musky aroma of this EO is less popular now. However, the EO obtained using a still of stainless steel has a lighter color and a sweeter, more subtle aroma than the EO obtained using a traditional iron still.

Price: $$

Peppermint Eucalyptus ct Piperitone (Eucalyptus dives ct piperitone)

Like all eucalyptus (whose properties and aroma can vary considerably), the peppermint eucalyptus tree is native to Australia. It also grows in South Africa. The EO is extracted from the leaves.

Properties

• antiseborrheic, dissolves grease

Uses

skin types: oily, prone to acne

hair types: oily

cellulite

This EO has a light menthol aroma. It is not recommended for young children or pregnant and nursing women.

Price: $

Petitgrain Bigarade (Citrus aurantium var. amara)

The bigarade orange tree (also known as the bitter orange or sour orange tree) is native to southern China. It was later introduced to the Mediterranean basin. It is now cultivated in all tropical and subtropical zones of the planet. The EO is extracted from the leaves.

Properties

• anti-inflammatory, regenerating, firming, healing, antibacterial, antiseborrheic, antiperspirant

Uses

skin types: oily, prone to acne, irritated, damaged

hair types: oily

eczema, excessive perspiration

The aroma of this EO recalls the aromas of orange peel essence and of the EO of the flower of the same tree (which is called Neroli oil), with a hint of green.

Price: $

Rock Rose or *Cistus (Cistus ladaniferus)*

This plant is native to the Mediterranean perimeter, and is mainly harvested in Spain where it grows wild. The EO is extracted from the branches and leaves (which are naturally covered with a perfumed resin, labdanum).

Properties

• excellent regenerating and anti-wrinkle properties, healing, astringent, toning, fights infection (viral, bacterial), coagulant

Uses

skin types: mature, wrinkled, prone to acne, damaged, dilated pores, stretch marks (preventive and curative)

minor wounds

This EO has a rather pronounced amber aroma (the oil from Morocco has an aroma quite a bit stronger than the oil from Provence). This EO has some of the best anti-wrinkle properties found among EOs.

Price: $$$

Rose (Rosa damascena)

Roses are native to the Middle East, and are now cultivated everywhere in the world. The Damask rose, which is much sought after for the production of EO, is now cultivated mainly in Bulgaria, Turkey, Iran, and North Africa. The EO is extracted from the flowers.

Properties

• astringent, regenerating, healing, firming

Uses

skin types: mature, wrinkled, prone to couperosis, sensitive, dry, damaged

The EO of rose has a delicate fragrance that is much sought after for the perfume industry. Since rose EO is very expensive, it is also of interest to use rose hydrosol, which is much less expensive.

Now stores carry a mixture composed of 10% rose EO and 90% vegetable oil, which allows one to obtain the benefits at a much more reasonable price.

This EO is often called the "queen of essential oils." It should not be confused with "rose otto" or "rose absolute," which is extracted by a chemical solvent and costs two to four times less than the EO. Rose otto is used in the perfume industry, but should not be used for skin and hair care products.

Price: $$$$$

Rosemary ct Verbenone (*Rosmarinus officinalis ct verbenoniferum*)

This shrub is native to the Mediterranean, where it is cultivated and grows wild. It is now found throughout Europe and the Americas. The EO is extracted from the flowering tops of the plant.

Properties

• highly regenerating and healing, excellent at controlling the production of sebum

Uses

skin types: dry, oily, mixed, prone to acne, mature, wrinkled, scars, stretch marks (healing)

hair types: oily, dry, dandruff

parasites (lice)

cellulite

Rosemary is a plant whose chemical composition can vary greatly depending on its conditions: land, sun, climate, altitude. Thus, the notion of chemotypes applies to rosemary. The EO that is of interest for skin and hair care products comes from plants that contain a large amount of verbenone, as identified by rigorous chemical analysis.

This EO should not be used by people with epilepsy or hormone-dependent cancer, by young children, or by pregnant or nursing women.

Price: $$

Rosewood (Aniba rosaeodora or A. parviflora)

This tree is native to Brazil and grows wild in the rain forest of the Amazonian basin (it should not be confused with the rosewood used for furniture, which is another species). Overexploitation and deforestation are threatening this species more and more. The EO is extracted from its wood and bark.

Properties

• astringent, fights infection (bacterial, fungal), regenerating

Uses

skin types: mature, wrinkled, prone to acne, dry, fragile, damaged

fungal infection of the skin

This EO has a sweet and agreeable aroma. It is usually well tolerated by all skin types. But, because of its high linalool content, it may cause allergic reactions.

Because of the threat of extinction, it is recommended that rosewood be used with moderation. Brazil, which is principal producer of rosewood in the world, now limits export and has set up a reforestation program for the EO that is certified organic. Note: Some rosewood EO that is found in stores is of poor quality and contains undesirable synthetic substances.

Price: $$

Sandalwood (Santalum Album)

This tree is native to southern India. It is also found in Indonesia and tropical zones of the Pacific Ocean. The EO is extracted from the wood at the core of the tree when the tree is between forty and eighty years old.

Properties

• regenerating, astringent, antibacterial, antifungal, healing, hydrating, anti-inflammatory

Uses

skin types: mature, wrinkled, dry, sensitive, damaged, chapped, prone to couperosis, dilated pores

This EO must be used in very small quantities in cosmetic preparations. At too high a concentration, it becomes harmful for the skin.

Because of overexploitation of this tree (it is also used for furniture), and because of the way the EO is extracted (which requires cutting the tree), the Sandalwood tree is seriously threatened with extinction. Buying the EO that comes from Asia is not recommended because of a lack of limits on harvesting. On the other hand, the EO that comes from New Caledonia (in the South Pacific) is recommended. It is extracted from the *Santalum austrocaledonicum* and is very much in demand for the finest perfumes. It is harvested in a much more ethical fashion: for each tree that is cut, three are planted. This will ensure the survival of the species.

This thick, dark yellow EO has a persistent woody aroma.

Price: $$$$

Sea Fennel (Crithmum maritimum)

This perennial plant is also known as samphire. It grows on the rocky coasts of western and southern Europe, from Scotland to the Mediterranean. The EO is extracted from the flowering tops of the plant.

Properties
- excellent regenerating and anti-wrinkle properties, firming, slimming (anti-cellulite)

Uses

skin types: mature, wrinkled, damaged, stretch marks

cellulite

This EO has a rather strong aroma that contains elements of
lemon and iodine.

Price: $$$

Tea Tree (Melaleuca alternifolia)

This tree is native to Australia, where it is now cultivated.
The EO is extracted from the leaves.

Properties

- excellent at fighting infection (bacterial, viral, fungal), cir-
culatory
- good at controlling dandruff

Uses

skin types: prone to acne, oily

hair types: dandruff

parasites (lice)

cold sores (labial herpes), fungal infection, varicose veins

This EO has a rather unpleasant odor, which is compensated
for by its effectiveness.

Price: $

Ylang-Ylang (Cananga odorata var. genuina)

This tree, which is native to Indonesia and the Philippines, is
cultivated in Asia, southern Africa, and the countries border-
ing the Indian Ocean. The EO is extracted from the flowers.

Properties

- anti-inflammatory, controls the production of sebum
- strengthening for the hair

Uses

skin types: oily, dry, mixed, prone to acne, irritated

hair types: oily, dry, hair loss

This EO is very effective at controlling acne. It can be applied directly and undiluted for this purpose, without causing a burning sensation.

The best-quality EO (C. *odorata v. genuina*) comes from the Indian Ocean, in particular, from the Comoro Islands, Mayotte (a French territory), and Madagascar. The medium-quality EO (C. *odorata v. macrophylla*) comes from Indonesia and the Philippines. The lowest-quality EO comes from China.

There are several grades of ylang-ylang EO that depend on when they were obtained during the distillation process. The two most sought-after grades are: "totum or complete" and "extra or extra superior." The less desirable grades are: "I, II, and III."

This EO has a very sweet, flowery aroma, which can be quite persistent.

Price: $$

Seven

Aromatic Hydrosols (AHs)

AHs are the condensate water co-produced during the steam distillation of plants. They contain volatile hydrophilic water-soluble aromatic molecules obtained from the plants. When they are sold, they may be called floral waters, hydrolats, herbal distillates, or aromatic waters. Regardless of the name used, it is important to verify that they are true AHs.

True AHs are obtained during the steam distillation of a plant. This process usually results in two complementary products: an essential oil and an AH. The AH is, in fact, the steam used to extract the essential oil during distillation. This steam, which contains certain aromatic molecules from the plant, condenses into water as it cools at the end of the distillation process. Like the essential oil, the AH is collected at the output of the still. The AH contains certain aromatic components of the plant and the essential oil in a naturally dissolved and less concentrated form.

As is the case for essential oils, the quality of an AH reflects the quality of the distillation—that it was done at a low temperature, at low pressure, and over a sufficiently long period of time.

There are more AHs than essential oils. Some plants are distilled specifically to obtain AHs, because they contain such a minute quantity of volatile aromatic molecules (not enough to produce essential oil). This is the case for cornflowers and for witch hazel, which are not, strictly speaking, aromatic plants.

As for essential oils, different parts of the plant (leaves, flowers, roots, bark) can be distilled.

For a long time, AHs were considered useless and without interest, except a few like rose water and orange blossom water. Fortunately, we are now discovering the virtues and properties of more and more of them.

The name *Neroli* comes from the princess of Nerola, a French aristocrat whose second marriage was to the Italian Flavio degli Orsini, the prince of Nerola. It was in Italy that she discovered the essential oil produced from the blossoms of the bitter orange tree. She developed a true passion for it. She perfumed her gloves with it and, in so doing, started a fashion that spread throughout the courts of seventeenth-century Europe. Since then, this essential oil has been known as Neroli oil.

AHs do not have the same aroma as the plant or the essential oil with which they are produced. This is because AHs are a concentrate of molecules that are hydrophilic (literally "water-loving"), whereas essential oils consist primarily of lipophilic (literally "fat-loving") aromatic molecules. The two types of products have different molecular compositions and aromas. AHs do not have the aromatic strength of essential oils, because the aromatic molecules are diluted in the distillation water. Certain AHs have a more herbaceous aroma than the corresponding essential oil, and others have an aroma surprisingly different from that of the essential oil. Some AHs have a distinctly unpleasant aroma, which does not in any way affect their virtues.

AHs have a relatively short shelf life when they are pure and do not contain preservatives (generally one year, but some AHs can be stored for as many as four years); it is, therefore, useless to buy them in large quantities. They must be kept cool and away from light and air—ideally they should be refrigerated, especially once the bottle has been opened. Good-quality AHs have an expiration date. You can limit their exposure to air and keep them longer by using them in a sterilized spray bottle—just transfer a small quantity of the AH to the spray bottle and keep the rest in the original bottle in the refrigerator. If an AH becomes cloudy or particles begin to form in it, it must no longer be used because bacteria are growing in it.

To prevent spoilage, to extend the shelf life, and to improve storage, some producers and distributors add preservatives in various amounts. These preservatives can be anything from alcohol (which is hard to detect in small quantities) to citrus seed extracts (which may or may not be organic) to chemical preservatives of various kinds (food preservatives and so on). AHs that are certified organic must not contain preservatives because no preservatives have been approved for use in AHs.

Certain practices result in products that are decidedly inferior or that have properties that are significantly different—in short, they result in products that have nothing to do with a true AH. It may be water to which a small quantity of essential oil has been added (along with a dispersal agent—like kaolin, talc, or magnesium—to emulsify it) and then filtered. Artificial aromas may also be added in order to give the product an aroma similar to that of the essential oil from the same plant, or another aroma that is simply more pleasant and attractive. These products should not be used for skin and hair care purposes.

As for floral infusions, they are made by soaking plant matter in water and then filtering the resulting infusion. They do not have the same composition or the same properties as the corresponding AHs, and they do not keep for very long.

Logically, plants or plant parts whose essence is obtained by mechanical expression cannot produce a true AH either. This is the case for citrus peels.

It is necessary to be vigilant and read labels carefully. The presence of the following information on a label indicates that the product is of a certain quality: the Latin name (which allows a more reliable identification of the plant used), the plant part that was distilled, the country of origin, production or expiration dates, or the presence or absence of preservatives and other foreign substances.

There are more than 500 species in the eucalyptus family. They can have very different components, properties, and aromas. Only a few are used for aromatherapy.

Some AHs, like certain essential oils, have been known since time immemorial for their cosmetic virtues (rose and witch hazel, for example). Others have only sparked interest in this domain much more recently. The gain in popularity of natural products in general and in aromatherapy in particular has contributed to this increase in interest.

Since AHs contain a lower concentration of aromatic molecules than do essential oils, they can be used with fewer precautions. They are very mild for the skin, they can be used pure, and they can be used to replace water with pleasing results.

If their cosmetic properties are very similar to those of the essential oil from the same plant, they are nonetheless not totally identical. Generally speaking, AHs are purifying and clarifying, anti-inflammatory, astringent, antiseptic, regenerating, good at controlling the production of sebum, healing, circulatory, calming, good at controlling dandruff, and stimulating for the scalp.

They can be used to clean the skin, as a skin toner, as an aftershave lotion, for hair care (as a final rinse after shampooing or as a daily spray), and in a mask or a cosmetic cream (as the aqueous phase).

The production costs are generally lower than those for essential oils (the difference is particularly significant for rose and Neroli AHs) because the yield is much higher. They provide a good way to benefit from certain properties of essential oils without spending a fortune.

In the following pages, you will find descriptions of twenty-one AHs. Some of them have just entered the world of dermocosmetics. It is getting easier and easier to find these AHs in stores—in particular, in stores carrying natural products. It may still be necessary to contact producers and distributors directly to find some of them.

Black Spruce (Picea mariana)

This resinous tree is native to Canada. The AH is produced from its needles.

Properties

• firming and toning for the breasts

Uses

lack of firmness of the breasts

The effect ends if one stops use for a few weeks.
It keeps for at least two years.

Carrot (Daucus carota)

The carrot is native to the Middle East and grows wild in uncultivated fields, on riverbanks, and by the roadside. The AH can be produced from the wild and cultivated varieties of carrot. It is produced from the seeds.

Properties

• regenerating, anti-inflammatory, calming

Uses

skin types: mature, irritated, prone to couperosis, wrinkled, damaged

psoriasis, eczema

This AH has an aroma similar to that of fresh carrots, with a hint of bitter chocolate.

It makes a good aftershave lotion.

It keeps for two years or more.

Cedar—Atlas (Cedrus atlantica), Cedar—Himalayan (Cedrus deodora)

The Atlas Cedar is native to North Africa. The Himalayan Cedar, as its name indicates, comes from the western Himalayas. The composition of the AHs produced from both species is almost identical. They are produced from the wood of the tree.

Properties

- astringent, antiseborrheic, circulatory, antibacterial, insecticide/insectifuge
- strengthening for the hair, good at controlling dandruff

Uses

skin types: oily, prone to acne, mature, damaged, wrinkled, prone to couperosis, dilated pores

hair types: oily, dull, dandruff, hair loss

parasites (lice)

eczema, psoriasis

This AH has a woody aroma.

It keeps for two years or more.

Note: Not to be confused with the various species of North American cedars (*Thuja, Juniperus, etc.*)

Chamomile—German (Matricaria recutita)

German chamomile, which is native to Europe and western Asia, is also known as blue chamomile. It grows by the roadside and in fields. It is also grown in gardens. The AH is produced from the flowers, which look like small daisies.

Properties

- highly anti-inflammatory, anti-allergic, healing, soothing, antiseptic

Uses

skin types: sensitive, irritated, prone to couperosis, prone to acne

irritated or slightly infected eyes

minor burns, insect bites, psoriasis, eczema, skin allergies

This AH is one of four existing ones that can be used as an eyewash.

It has an herbaceous aroma, with a hint of the infusion of the same plant.

It makes a good aftershave lotion.

Its shelf life is one and a half to two years.

Chamomile—Roman (Chamaemelum nobile)

Roman chamomile is native to western Europe and North Africa. It is fond of dry fields and cultivated land. The AH is produced from the white flowers.

Properties

- highly anti-inflammatory, calming, astringent, regenerating, softening

Uses

skin types: oily (in combination with the AH of neroli), dry, sensitive, irritated, prone to acne, prone to couperosis, mature (in combination with the AH of witch hazel), dilated pores

irritated and slightly infected eyes

minor burns, eczema, psoriasis, skin allergies, insect bites and stings

This AH is one of four existing ones that can be used as an eyewash.

Due to its considerable astringent properties, it is preferable to avoid using it alone on very dry skin for an extended period.

Its aroma is both herbaceous and delicately flowery.

It keeps very well for two years or more.

Cornflower (Centaurea cyanus)

The cornflower is native to the Near East and is very common throughout Europe, Asia, and North America, where it grows freely in cultivated fields and in meadows. The AH is produced from the flowers.

Properties

- purifying, anti-inflammatory, decongestant, astringent, firming, clarifying for the complexion
- strengthening for the hair

Uses

skin types: mature, dry, irritated, damaged, fine wrinkles (in combination with the AH of rock rose), dilated pores, sallow complexion

irritated or swollen eyes

hair types: dull, damaged

This AH is one of four existing ones that can be used as an eyewash.

It has a light herbaceous aroma.

Its shelf life is about one year.

Geranium or Rose Geranium (Pelargonium x asperum)

The geranium, which is native to South Africa, is now cultivated in the entire world. The AH is produced from the leaves.

Properties

- controls the production of sebum, hydrating, coagulant, anti-inflammatory, antiperspirant

Uses

skin types: oily, dry, mixed, prone to couperosis, prone to acne, wrinkled, irritated

hair types: oily, dry, dandruff

wounds and minor cuts, excessive perspiration

This AH has a delicate aroma that is reminiscent of roses.

Its composition varies greatly depending on where it was cultivated. The EO of plants cultivated on l'Île de la Réunion (cv Bourbon) and in North Africa (cv Egypt) are of the greatest interest and the most sought-after. The composition and properties of the EO from China (cv China) and from Russia (cv Russia) are different. (Cv means "cultivar" and designates a plant that has been deliberately selected for its specificity—in this case, its particular aromatic molecules.)

It makes a good aftershave lotion.

It keeps for one year to eighteen months.

Helichrysum (Helichrysum italicum)

This plant is part of the everlasting family and is native to the Mediterranean basin. In particular, it is found in Corsica (the most sought-after quality), where it grows wild, as well as the Balkan region (Italy, Bosnia, etc.). The AH is produced from the flowers.

Properties

- highly healing and circulatory, astringent, regenerating, soothing, anti-inflammatory

Uses

skin types: prone to couperosis, irritated, sensitive, mature, wrinkled, damaged, scars, dilated pores

circles under the eyes

eczema, bruises

The great demand for this AH worldwide has led to its scarcity and, since 2007, to its cultivation, especially in Corsica.

It has an unusual aroma that is reminiscent of hay.

It keeps for two years.

Lavender—True (Lavandula angustifolia or *L. officinalis* or *L. vera*)

True lavender is native to the mountainous zones of the western Mediterranean. It has become a symbol of southwestern France. The AH is produced from the flowering tops.

Properties

• antiseptic, healing, softening, astringent, anti-inflammatory, soothing, insecticide/insectifuge

Uses

skin types: oily, mixed, sensitive, damaged, prone to acne, irritated, dilated pores

hair types: oily, dull

lice (preventive)

minor burns and wounds, insect bites

This AH has an herbaceous aroma, with a hint of flowers that is vaguely reminiscent of the essential oil from the same plant.

It makes a good aftershave lotion.

It keeps two years or more.

Lemon Balm or Melissa (*Melissa officinalis*)

This plant is native to the eastern Mediterranean basin. It is now cultivated around the world. The AH is produced from the leaves and stalks before they blossom.

Properties

- anti-inflammatory, antioxidant, astringent, soothing, antiviral, dandruff

Uses

skin types: oily, prone to acne, irritated, sensitive, sallow complexion, dilated pores

hair types: dandruff

eczema, skin allergies, cold sores (labial herpes)

Since the essential oil of melissa is very expensive and can irritate the skin, the AH is a good alternative.

It has a light floral aroma.

It keeps for two years or more.

Lemon Verbena (*Aloysia citriodora* or *Lippia citriodora*)

This perennial shrub is native to South America. It is grown in all temperate climates. The AH is produced from the leaves.

Properties

• anti-inflammatory, clarifying, toning, firming

Uses

skin types: oily, dry, mixed, irritated, sallow complexion, dilated
   pores

Since the essential oil of lemon verbena is very expensive and
   can irritate the skin, the AH is a good alternative.

It has a delicate, slightly lemony aroma.

It keeps for twelve to eighteen months or more.

Neroli (Citrus aurantium var. amara)

The bigarade orange tree, also known as the bitter or sour orange tree, is native to southern China. It was later introduced
to the Mediterranean basin, and is now cultivated in all tropical and subtropical zones of the planet. The AH is produced
from the flowers (and is also known as orange blossom AH).

Properties

• circulatory, astringent, anti-inflammatory, somewhat antibacterial, soothing, calming

Uses

skin types: mature, sensitive, irritated, prone to acne, oily, prone
   to couperosis, dry, dilated pores

This AH is useful for dry skin, which it relaxes and softens;
   however, it is not recommended for very dry skin.

Since neroli essential oil is very expensive, the AH is a good
   alternative.

It has a delicate floral aroma that is slightly acidic.

It keeps for two years or more.

Rock Rose or Labdanum (Cistus ladaniferus)

This plant is native to the Mediterranean perimeter, and is mainly harvested in Spain, where it grows wild. The AH is produced from the branches and leaves (which are naturally covered with a perfumed resin, labdanum).

Properties

• excellent regenerating and anti-wrinkle properties, toning, astringent, healing, coagulant, fights infection (bacterial, viral)

Uses

skin types: mature, damaged, wrinkled, prone to acne, dilated pores, scars, cuts and minor wounds

This AH has a rather unusual herbaceous aroma with a hint of amber. It is not always considered pleasant.

It makes a good aftershave lotion.

It keeps for two years or more.

Rose (Rosa damascena)

Roses are native to the Middle East, and are now cultivated everywhere in the world. The Damask rose, which is much sought-after for the production of essential oil, is now cultivated mainly in Bulgaria, Turkey, Iran, and North Africa. The AH is produced from the flowers.

Properties

- regenerating, soothing, toning, astringent, controls the production of sebum, antibacterial, hydrating, softening, anti-inflammatory

Uses

skin types: dry, oily, mixed, mature, sensitive, dull, prone to couperosis, prone to acne, sallow complexion, dilated pores

hair types: oily, dry, damaged

Used in combination with the rock rose, whose aroma it greatly improves, this AH helps prevent wrinkles and is a real pick-me-up for the skin.

Since rose essential oil is very expensive, the AH is a good alternative.

It has a lovely sweet rose aroma (especially when produced from fresh petals).

It keeps for two years.

Rosemary ct Verbenone (Rosmarinus officinalis ct verbenoniferum)

This shrub is native to the Mediterranean, where it is cultivated and grows wild. It is now found throughout Europe and the Americas. The AH produced from the flowering tops of the plant.

Properties

- purifying (helps bring impurities to the surface of the skin and unblock the pores), firming, regenerating, controls the production of sebum, antioxidant, antiseptic, soothing, softening, dandruff, strengthening for the hair

Uses

skin types: dry, oily, mixed, irritated, prone to acne, mature, damaged, sallow complexion, blackheads

hair types: oily, dull, hair loss, dandruff

Rosemary is a plant whose chemical composition can vary greatly depending on its conditions: land, sun, climate, altitude. Thus, the notion of chemotypes applies to rosemary. The AH that is of interest for cosmetic purposes comes from plants that contain a large amount of verbenone, as identified by rigorous chemical analysis.

It has a mildly herbaceous aroma, which is less intense than that of the plant.

It keeps for twelve to eighteen months.

Witch Hazel (Hamamelis virginiana)

This tree is native to North America. The AH is produced from its leaves and branches.

Properties

• astringent, healing, antioxidant, antiseptic, soothing, dandruff, decongestant, circulatory, anti-inflammatory

Uses

skin types: oily, dry, mixed, prone to couperosis, prone to acne, mature, irritated, sensitive, dilated pores

hair types: dandruff

insect bites, eczema, psoriasis

This AH is very mild for the skin.

It has an herbaceous aroma with a hint of woodiness.

The AH that is found in stores these days often contains pre-servatives. Be careful!

It keeps for eight to twelve months.

Yarrow (Achillea millefolium)

There are several breeds of yarrow that grow wild in all temperate zones of the world. Some originate from North America, others from Europe or Asia. Most of the yarrows found in North America are a complex of both native and introduced plants.Its Latin name comes from Achilles, the mythical Greek character who was supposed to have used it to heal soldiers' wounds. The AH is produced from the top growth of the plant when it is in flower.

Properties

• astringent, anti-inflammatory, antibacterial, coagulant, antiseborrheic
• strengthening for the hair

Uses

skin types: prone to acne, oily, irritated, prone to couperosis, dilated pores

hair types: oily, dull

eczema, psoriasis, minor wounds

This AH has a light aroma that is not always considered pleasant (and can be masked by carrot AH).

Its shelf life is about two years.

Here are a few more hydrosols that are useful for hair care:

Juniper (Juniperus communis): oily hair

Scotch Pine (Pinus sylvestris): oily hair

Golden Rod (Solidago canadensis): dull or damaged hair

Eight

Some Emulsifiers

For people who wish to begin preparing creams and milks, this section contains information about a number of emulsifiers. Some are readily available. Others can only be found in specialty shops.

BEESWAX

This natural product is made by honey bees. Its composition is complex and it contains many different constituents. Unrefined beeswax is yellow or amber in color, solid at room temperature, and slightly sticky. It has an agreeable aroma that smells like honey.

Beeswax makes the skin softer and more supple. It is also anti-inflammatory and antibacterial. It takes a long time to be absorbed by the skin, and forms a protective film on the skin that slows the loss of humidity. It must be used in small quantities to ensure it does not block the pores or make the preparation too sticky.

It is used primarily as a thickening agent for ointments and lip balms. Unfortunately, it is a poor emulsifier—the two phases (oily and aqueous) of a preparation tend to separate quickly. Adding a small amount of borax stabilizes emulsions that include beeswax (the amount of borax can be up to one-eighteenth of the amount of beeswax).

Beeswax is melted in the oil phase of the emulsion. It can make up 2 to 10% of the total weight of all ingredients in a preparation. Grate the beeswax in order to make it easier to weigh and melt.

Unrefined beeswax can be found in stores carrying natural products.

BORAX

Borax is a natural mineral that generally comes in the form of a white powder or crystals.

In addition to being an emulsifier, it also has antibacterial and antifungal properties. It is especially good at stabilizing emulsions that include beeswax.

It is drying, irritating, and potentially allergenic for the skin.

Incorporate it into the aqueous phase of the emulsion. It can make up 0.5% of the total weight of all ingredients in a preparation. Since the amount of borax incorporated is so minute, it is not counted in the percentage of emulsifiers in a preparation.

Borax can be found in pharmacies and supermarkets.

CETYL ALCOHOL

This fatty alcohol is naturally present in vegetable and animal fats. The cetyl alcohol from vegetable sources, of interest here, comes mainly from palm kernel oil, palm oil, and coconut oil. In the past, it was extracted from the fat of cetaceans (spermaceti). It generally comes in the form of waxy granules.

It stabilizes and thickens emulsions, giving them a creamy, unctuous texture.

It is incorporated (together with another emulsifier) into the oil phase of the emulsion. It can make up 2 to 5% of the total weight of all ingredients in a preparation.

It can replace beeswax in ointments.

It softens the skin, but may be irritating for people with sensitive skin.

Cetyl alcohol can be found in stores that specialize in ingredients for skin and hair care.

EMULSIFYING WAX

This term is used for a wide variety of products composed of ingredients that may be from vegetable sources or may be derived from petroleum.

Emulsifying wax does not exist in a natural state. It is very difficult, if not impossible, to know the techniques and the exact ingredients involved in manufacturing the many types of emulsifying wax that are available on the market ("it's a trade secret").

By using emulsifying wax, it is easy to prepare very stable emulsions.

GUM TRAGACANTH

This substance is made from the dried sap of a shrub in the *Astragalus* family, which is native to the Middle East. It is also known as tragacanth and gum dragon. It is a gelling agent that thickens and emulsifies. It is also used in many foods and pharmaceuticals. It comes in the form of a beige powder or flakes.

It is dissolved in the aqueous phase of an emulsion. It can make up 0.5 to 2% of the total weight of all ingredients in a preparation. Since it must be dissolved in a boiling liquid, it is not recommended for hydrosols that are degraded by heat.

Gum tragacanth can be obtained from suppliers who specialize in ingredients for pastries.

GUM ARABIC

Also known as acacia gum, this gum is made from the sap of certain species of acacia tree that grow in dry tropical regions, especially in Africa. It emulsifies, but does not thicken. Because of these properties, it is also used in the food and pharmaceutical industries. It is used traditionally to treat skin conditions. It comes in the form of a white powder.

It is dissolved in the aqueous phase of an emulsion—the aqueous phase does not need to be heated. It can make up 1 to 10% of the total weight of all ingredients in a preparation.

Gum arabic can be found in oriental grocery stores and in stores specializing in ingredients for pastries.

GUM XANTHAN

This ingredient is produced by the fermentation of sugar with a bacteria. It is used to thicken and stabilize emulsions. It is also used in the food industry because of these properties. It comes in the form of a white powder.

It is dissolved in the aqueous phase of an emulsion—the aqueous phase does not need to be heated. It can make up 0.5 to 2% of the total weight of all ingredients in a preparation.

Xanthan gum can be found in pharmacies and in stores specializing in natural products.

STEARIC ACID OR STEARIN

This fatty acid is naturally present in vegetable and animal fats (cocoa butter contains about 30% stearic acid). The stearic acid from vegetable sources of interest here comes mainly from palm oil, palm kernel oil, coconut oil, and soya oil. Generally, it comes in the form of waxy granules.

It stabilizes and thickens emulsions, giving them a creamy, unctuous texture.

It is incorporated into the oil phase of an emulsion. It can make up 2 to 10% of the total weight of all ingredients in a preparation. Note: If the proportion is increased, the preparation will be pasty.

It can also replace beeswax in ointments.

Stearic acid can be found in stores that specialize in ingredients for skin and hair care.

SOYA LECITHIN (LIQUID)

This is a pasty yellowish-brown liquid. The lecithin is extracted by pressing at the same time as soya oil; it is then separated from the oil by settling. Unfortunately, it can also be extracted by the use of chemical solvents (be sure to check the quality of the product before buying it).

It is a natural emulsifier and thickener that gives an unctuous texture to preparations.

It also nourishes, softens, and hydrates the skin.

It is incorporated into the oil phase of an emulsion. It can make up 2 to 5% of the total weight of all ingredients in a preparation.

Soya lecithin can be found in stores specializing in natural products.

Nine

Conclusion

As you can see, nature has a lot to offer us!

It is really possible to prepare great skin care products for various needs and puposes, and to do it a simple way. It is also a good opportunity to get away from some of the synthetic chemicals that many common products contain.

Because natural products are very fashionable these days, much research is being conducted in this field and into other new ingredients; new data will undoubtedly become available to the public. This will continue to expand the possibilities of homemade skin and hair care products.

Enjoy the pleasure of discovering new ingredients, planning and preparing your own recipes, and finally, using your great, homemade, completely personalized products.

And be careful—once immersed in the world of natural aromas, using synthetic ones becomes less desirable and you'll find yourself making more of your own skin and hair care products!

THREE

The

Appendices

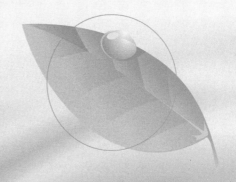

Appendix 1: Properties Index

PROPERTIES

Analgesic

VO: tamanu

EO: blue tansy, Roman chamomile, spike lavender, true lavender

Anti-allergic

EO: blue tansy, German chamomile

AH: German chamomile

Antibacterial, anti-infectious, antiseptic

VO: karanja, neem, nigella, sea buckthorn, tamanu

IO: comfrey, plantain, calendula

EO: Atlas Cedar, benzoin, cypress, geranium, green myrtle, helichrysum, palmarosa, petitgrain bigarade, rock rose, rosewood, sandalwood, spike lavender, tea tree, true lavender, bay rum, myrrh

AH: Atlas Cedar, German chamomile, neroli, rock rose, rose, rosemary ct verbenone, true lavender, witch hazel, yarrow

Anticoagulant

EO: helichrysum

Antifungal

VO: castor, neem, nigella

EO: benzoin, geranium, palmarosa, sandalwood, spike lavender, tea tree

Anti-inflammatory

VO: wheat germ, neem, nigella, raspberry seed, rice bran, sea buckthorn, tamanu, jojoba

VB: shea

IO: calendula, plantain

EO: benzoin, blue tansy, clary sage, Eastern Red Cedar, geranium, German chamomile, helichrysum, myrrh, patchouli, petitgrain bigarade, Roman chamomile, sandalwood, true lavender, ylang-ylang

AH: carrot, cornflower, geranium, German chamomile, helichrysum, lemon verbena, lemon balm, neroli, Roman chamomile, rose, true lavender, witch hazel, yarrow

Antioxidant

VO: camellia, rice bran

AH: lemon balm, rosemary ct verbenone, witch hazel

Antiperspirant

EO: clary sage, cypress, geranium, petitgrain bigarade

AH: geranium

Antipigmentation

VO: castor, musk rose

IO: comfrey, white lily

EO: celery

Antitoxic

EO: spike lavender

Astringent

VO: grape seed, hazelnut

EO: Atlas Cedar, clary sage, cypress, Eastern Red Cedar, geranium, green myrtle, helichrysum,neroli, palmarosa, patchouli, rock rose, rose, rosewood, sandalwood, true lavender

AH: Atlas Cedar, cornflower, helichrysum, lemon balm,
neroli, Roman chamomile, rock rose, rose, true lavender,
witch hazel, yarrow

Circulatory

VO: tamanu

IO: calendula

EO: Atlas Cedar, benzoin, cypress, Eastern Red Cedar, green
myrtle, helichrysum, neroli, patchouli, tea tree

AH: Atlas Cedar, helichrysum, neroli, witch hazel

Coagulant

EO: geranium, rock rose

AH: geranium, rock rose, yarrow

Dandruff (controlling)

EO: Atlas Cedar, tea tree, bay rum

AH: Atlas Cedar, lemon balm, rosemary ct verbenone, witch hazel

Decongestant

AH: cornflower, witch hazel

Firming, toning (skin)

VO: apricot kernel, argan, avocado, hazelnut, hemp, sweet almond

VB: kokum

EO: carrot, geranium, green myrtle, petitgrain bigarade, rock rose, rose, sea fennel

AH: cornflower, lemon verbena, rock rose, rose, rosemary ct verbenone

Firming (breasts)

IO: daisy

EO: black spruce

AH: black spruce

Healing

VO: argan, castor, hemp, macadamia, musk rose, sesame, marula, nigella, raspberry seed, sea buckthorn, tamanu

VB: mango, shea

IO: calendula, comfrey, plantain, white lily

EO: Atlas Cedar, benzoin, carrot, geranium, German chamomile, helichrysum, myrrh, neroli, palmarosa, petitgrain bigarade, rock rose, rose, rosemary ct verbenone, sandalwood, spike lavender, true lavender

AH: German chamomile, helichrysum, rock rose, true lavender, witch hazel

Hydrating

VO: avocado

EO: myrrh, palmarosa

AH: geranium, rose, sandalwood

Insecticide/insectifuge (mosquitoes, lices,etc.)

VO: karanja, neem

EO: Atlas Cedar, geranium, true lavender

AH: Atlas Cedar, true lavender

Nourishing

VO: apricot kernel, castor, hazelnut, macadamia, olive, sunflower, babassu, baobab, camelina, camellia, meadowfoam, marula, prickly pear, rice bran

VB: cocoa, illipe and sal, mango, shea

Protective

VO: argan, avocado, hazelnut, jojoba, macadamia, camelina, cranberry seed, kukui, meadowfoam, marula, prickly pear, rice bran, sea buckthorn

VB: cocoa, coconut, illipe and sal, shea

IO: carrot

Purifying, clarifying

VO: hazelnut

AH: cornflower, lemon verbena, rosemary ct verbenone

Regenerating

VO: apricot kernel, argan, avocado, borage, evening prim-rose, grape seed, hemp, jojoba, macadamia, musk rose, sesame, wheat germ, baobab, camellia, cranberry seed, karanja, kukui, marula, meadowfoam, neem, nigella, prickly pear, raspberry seed, sea buckthorn, tamanu, watermelon seed

VB: coconut, kokum, shea

IO: calendula, carrot, comfrey, white lily

EO: benzoin, carrot, clary sage, helichrysum, myrrh, neroli, palmarosa, patchouli, petitgrain bigarade, rock rose, rose, rosemary ct verbenone, rosewood, sandalwood, sea fennel, spike lavender, true lavender

AH: carrot, helichrysum, Roman chamomile, rock rose, rose, rosemary ct verbenone

Sebum (controlling), antiseborrheic

VO: hazelnut, jojoba, meadowfoam, watermelon seed

EO: Atlas Cedar, clary sage, cypress, Eastern Red Cedar, green myrtle, palmarosa, petitgrain bigarade, peppermint eucalyptus, rosemary ct verbenone, ylang-ylang

AH: Atlas Cedar, geranium, rose, rosemary ct verbenone, yarrow

Slimming (anti-cellulite)
EO: sea fennel

Softening
VO: apricot kernel, argan, borage, castor, evening primrose, hemp, jojoba, macadamia, olive, prickly pear, sesame, sunflower, sweet almond, wheat germ, babassu, baobab, camelina, camellia, cranberry seed, kukui, meadowfoam, nigella, raspberry seed, rice bran, sea buckthorn

VB: cocoa, coconut, illipe and sal, kokum, mango, shea

IO: calendula, carrot, white lily

AH: Roman chamomile, rose, rosemary ct verbenone, true lavender

Soothing, calming
VO: jojoba, macadamia, olive, sesame, sweet almond, wheat germ, kukui, marula, meadowfoam

VB: coconut

IO: calendula, comfrey, plantain, white lily

EO: blue tansy, neroli

AH: carrot, German chamomile, helichrysum, lemon balm, neroli, Roman chamomile, rose, rosemary ct verbenone, true lavender, witch hazel

Strengthening (hair)

VO: camelina, camellia, castor, cranberry seed, kukui, nigella, raspberry seed, sea buckthorn, prickly pear

VB: shea

EO: Atlas Cedar, clary sage, ylang-ylang, bay rum

AH: Atlas cedar, cornflower, rosemary ct verbenone, yarrow

Sunscreen

VO: apricot kernel, jojoba, sesame, wheat germ, cranberry seed, raspberry seed, sea buckthorn

VB: mango, shea

Supple (make more)

VO: argan, avocado, borage, evening primrose, hazelnut, musk rose, sunflower, sweet almond, marula, watermelon seed

VB: cocoa, coconut, illipe and sal, kokum, mango, shea

IO: carrot

Appendix 2: Usage Index

THE SKIN

Acne

VO: argan, hemp, jojoba, musk rose, karanja, kukui, neem, nigella, raspberry seed, sea buckthorn, tamanu

VB: kokum

IO: calendula, carrot, comfrey, plantain

EO: Atlas cedar, bay rum, benzoin, carrot, clary sage, Eastern Red Cedar, geranium, German chamomile, green myrtle, helichrysum, myrrh, palmarosa, patchouli, peppermint eucalyptus, petitgrain bigarade, rock rose, Roman chamomile, rosemary ct verbenone, spike lavender, rosewood, tea tree, true lavender, ylang-ylang

AH: Atlas cedar, geranium, German chamomile, lemon balm, neroli, Roman chamomile, rock rose, rose, rosemary ct verbenone, true lavender, witch hazel, yarrow

Blackheads

VO: hazelnut

AH: rosemary ct verbenone

Chapped

VO: argan, avocado, macadamia, sweet almond, wheat germ, baobab, kukui, tamanu

VB: shea, cocoa

IO: calendula, carrot, comfrey

EO: benzoin, palmarosa, sandalwood, spike lavender

Complexion (sallow)

IO: white lily

AH: cornflower, lemon verbena, lemon balm, rose, rosemary ct verbenone

Couperosis

VO: musk rose, tamanu

IO: calendula, white lily

EO: Atlas Cedar, bay rum, benzoin, blue tansy, carrot, cypress, Eastern Red Cedar, German chamomile, green myrtle, helichrysum, myrrh, neroli, patchouli, Roman chamomile, rose, sandalwood, true lavender

AH: Atlas Cedar, carrot, geranium, German chamomile, helichrysum, neroli, Roman chamomile, rose, witch hazel, yarrow

Damaged

VO: apricot kernel, argan, avocado, borage, evening primrose, grape seed, hazelnut, hemp, macadamia, musk rose,
wheat germ, baobab, camellia, cranberry seed, karanja,
kukui, marula, meadowfoam, neem, nigella, prickly pear,
raspberry seed, sea buckthorn, tamanu, watermelon seed

VB: coconut, kokum, shea

IO: calendula, comfrey, plantain

EO: carrot, geranium, green myrtle, helichrysum, palmarosa,
patchouli, petitgrain bigarade, rock rose, rose, rosemary ct
verbenone, rosewood, sandalwood, sea fennel, spike lavender, true lavender

AH: Atlas Cedar, carrot, cornflower, helichrysum, rock rose,
rosemary ct verbenone, true lavender

Dry

VO: apricot kernel, argan, avocado, borage, castor, evening
primrose, hazelnut, hemp, jojoba, macadamia, musk rose,
olive, sesame, sunflower, sweet almond, wheat germ, babassu, baobab, camelina, camellia, cranberry seed, kukui,
marula, meadowfoam, neem, nigella, prickly pear, raspberry seed, rice bran, sea buckthorn, tamanu

VB: cocoa, coconut, illipe and sal, kokum, mango, shea

IO: calendula

EO: benzoin, carrot, geranium, green myrtle, myrrh, neroli,
palmarosa, patchouli, rose, rosemary ct verbenone, rosewood, sandalwood, ylang-ylang

AH: cornflower, geranium, lemon verbena, neroli, Roman
chamomile, rose, rosemary ct verbenone, witch hazel

Exposure to elements (protection)

VO: apricot kernel, argan, avocado, jojoba, sesame, wheat germ, camelina, cranberry seed, meadowfoam, raspberry seed, sea buckthorn

VB: cocoa, illipe and sal, mango, shea

IO: carrot

Irritated

VO: hazelnut, macadamia, olive, sesame, sweet almond, babassu, camellia, kukui, marula, meadowfoam, neem, nigella, raspberry seed, rice bran, sea buckthorn, tamanu

VB: shea

IO: calendula, comfrey, plantain, white lily

EO: benzoin, blue tansy, geranium, German chamomile, green myrtle, myrrh, neroli, palmarosa, patchouli, petitgrain bigarade, Roman chamomile, true lavender, ylang-ylang

AH: carrot, cornflower, geranium, German chamomile, helichrysum, lemon verbena, lemon balm, neroli, Roman chamomile, rosemary ct verbenone, true lavender, witch hazel, yarrow

Mixed

VO: apricot kernel, argan, grape seed, hazelnut, hemp, jojoba, macadamia, musk rose, babassu, camellia, kukui, meadowfoam, prickly pear, raspberry seed, rice bran, tamanu, watermelon seed

EO: geranium, green myrtle, palmarosa, rosemary ct verbenone, ylang-ylang

AH: geranium, lemon verbena, rose, rosemary ct verbenone, true lavender, witch hazel

Oily

VO: grape seed, hazelnut, jojoba, meadowfoam, watermelon seed, apricot kernel, argan, hemp, macadamia, musk rose, babassu, camellia, kukui, prickly pear, raspberry seed, rice bran, tamanu

EO: Atlas Cedar, clary sage, cypress, Eastern Red Cedar, geranium, green myrtle, neroli, palmarosa, peppermint eucalyptus, petitgrain bigarade, rosemary ct verbenone, spike lavender, tea tree, true lavender, ylang-ylang

AH: Atlas Cedar, geranium, lemon verbena, lemon balm, neroli, Roman chamomile, rose, rosemary ct verbenone, true lavender, witch hazel, yarrow

Pigmentation spots

VO: castor, musk rose, camellia

IO: comfrey, white lily

EO: carrot, celery

Pores (dilated)

VO: grape seed, hazelnut

EO: Eastern Red Cedar, geranium, green myrtle, helichrysum, palmarosa, patchouli, rock rose, sandalwood, true lavender

AH: Atlas Cedar, cornflower, helichrysum, lemon verbena, lemon balm, neroli, rock rose, Roman chamomile, rose, true lavender, witch hazel, yarrow

Sensitive, fragile

VO: avocado, hazelnut, jojoba, macadamia, prickly pear, camelina, kukui, rice bran

VB: coconut, kokum

IO: calendula, carrot, plantain

EO: German chamomile, neroli, Roman chamomile, rose, rosewood, sandalwood

AH: German chamomile, helichrysum, lemon balm, neroli, Roman chamomile, rose, true lavender, witch hazel

Scars

VO: argan, macadamia, musk rose, sea buckthorn, tamanu

VB: shea

IO: calendula, comfrey

EO: helichrysum, palmarosa, rock rose, rosemary ct verbenone, true lavender

AH: helichrysum, rock rose

Stretch marks

VO: argan, musk rose, macadamia, wheat germ, baobab, camelina

VB: shea

EO: geranium, green myrtle, helichrysum, rock rose, sea fennel, spike lavender, rosemary ct verbenone, true lavender

Wrinkled, mature

VO: apricot kernel, argan, avocado, borage, evening primrose, grape seed, hazelnut, hemp, jojoba, macadamia, olive, musk rose, wheat germ, baobab, camellia, camelina, cranberry seed, karanja, kukui, marula, meadowfoam, nigella, prickly pear, raspberry seed, rice bran, sea buckthorn, tamanu, watermelon seed

VB: cocoa, coconut, kokum, mango, illipe and sal, shea

IO: calendula, white lily

EO: benzoin, carrot, clary sage, geranium, green myrtle, helichrysum, myrrh, neroli, palmarosa, patchouli, rock rose, rose, rosemary ct verbenone, rosewood, sandalwood, sea fennel

AH: Atlas Cedar, carrot, cornflower, geranium, helichrysum, neroli, rock rose, Roman chamomile, rose, rosemary ct verbenone, witch hazel

THE EYES

Circles (under the eyes)

EO: Atlas Cedar, cypress, Eastern Red Cedar, helichrysum

AH: helichrysum

Infected (slightly)

AH: German chamomile, Roman chamomile

Irritated

AH: cornflower, German chamomile, Roman chamomile

Swollen

AH: cornflower

THE BREASTS

Lack of firmness

IO: daisy

EO: black spruce

AH: black spruce

THE HAIR

Damaged, brittle, dull

VO: apricot kernel, argan, avocado, borage, castor, evening primrose, grape seed, hazelnut, hemp, kukui, macadamia, olive, musk rose, sesame, babassu, camelina, camellia, cranberry seed, marula, meadowfoam, neem, nigella, prickly pear, raspberry seed, rice bran, watermelon seed

VB: coconut, kokum, mango, illipe and sal, shea

IO: calendula

EO: Atlas Cedar, bay rum, ylang-ylang

AH: Atlas Cedar, cornflower, golden rod, rose, rosemary ct verbenone, true lavender, yarrow

Dandruff

VO: camellia, cranberry seed, neem, sea buckthorn

EO: Atlas Cedar, bay rum, clary sage, geranium, palmarosa, patchouli, rosemary ct verbenone, tea tree

AH: Atlas Cedar, geranium, lemon balm, rosemary ct verbenone, witch hazel

Dry

VO: apricot kernel, argan, avocado, borage, castor, evening primrose, hazelnut, hemp, jojoba, macadamia, olive, ses-

ame, sunflower, wheat germ, babassu, baobab, camelina,
camellia, marula, meadowfoam, prickly pear, rice bran, sea
buckthorn

VB: coconut, kokum, mango, illipe and sal, shea

IO: calendula

EO: bay rum, green myrtle, palmarosa, rosemary ct verbenone, ylang-ylang

AH: geranium, rose

Hair loss

VO: apricot kernel, castor, kukui, nigella, raspberry seed, sea
buckthorn

EO: Atlas Cedar, bay rum, clary sage, ylang-ylang

AH: Atlas Cedar, rosemary ct verbenone

Oily

VO: grape seed, hazelnut, jojoba, meadowfoam, watermelon
seed

EO: Atlas Cedar, bay rum, cypress, Eastern Red Cedar, green
myrtle, palmarosa, peppermint eucalyptus, petitgrain bigarade, rosemary ct verbenone, ylang-ylang

AH: Atlas Cedar, geranium, juniper, rose, rosemary ct verbenone, scotch-pine, true lavender, yarrow

Parasites (lice)

VO: karanja, neem

EO: Atlas Cedar, geranium, green myrtle, rosemary ct verbenone, tea tree, true lavender

AH: Atlas Cedar, true lavender

THE NAILS

Brittle

VO: borage, castor, olive, baobab

MINOR SKIN PROBLEMS

Allergies

IO: carrot

EO: blue tansy, German chamomile, patchouli, Roman chamomile

AH: German chamomile, lemon balm, Roman chamomile

Bruises

EO: helichrysum

AH: helichrysum

Burns and wounds (minor)

VO: argan, musk rose, sweet almond, kukui, tamanu, nigella, sea buckthorn

VB: kokum, shea

IO: calendula, comfrey, plantain

EO: benzoin, geranium, German chamomile, myrrh, palmarosa, rock rose, Roman chamomile, spike lavender, true lavender

AH: geranium, German chamomile, rock rose, Roman chamomile, true lavender, yarrow

Cellulite

EO: Atlas Cedar, helichrysum, peppermint eucalyptus, rosemary ct verbenone, sea fennel

Cold sores (labial herpes)

VO: neem, tamanu

EO: green myrtle, helichrysum, palmarosa, spike lavender, tea tree

AH: lemon balm

Eczema, psoriasis

VO: avocado, borage, evening primrose, hemp, musk rose, wheat germ, babassu, baobab, camelina, cranberry seed, karanja, kukui, neem, nigella, raspberry seed, sea buckthorn, tamanu

VB: shea

IO: calendula, carrot, comfrey, plantain

EO: Atlas Cedar, blue tansy, carrot, geranium, German chamomile, helichrysum, myrrh, palmarosa, patchouli, petitgrain bigarade, Roman chamomile, spike lavender, true lavender

AH: Atlas Cedar, carrot, German chamomile, helichrysum, lemon balm, Roman chamomile, witch hazel, yarrow

Fungus

VO: castor, neem, nigella

IO: calendula

EO: benzoin, geranium, myrrh, palmarosa, rosewood, spike lavender, tea tree

Insect bites and stings

IO: calendula, plantain

EO: blue tansy, spike lavender, true lavender

AH: German chamomile, Roman chamomile, true lavender, witch hazel

Perspiration (excessive)

EO: clary sage, cypress, geranium, petitgrain bigarade

AH: geranium

Varicose veins

VO: tamanu

IO: calendula

EO: Atlas Cedar, cypress, Eastern Red Cedar, green myrtle, helichrysum, patchouli, tea tree

Appendix 3: English Lexicon

CLASSIC VEGETABLE OILS

English	*Latin*	French
Apricot kernel	*Prunus armeniaca*	Noyau d'abricot
Argan/Argania	*Argania spinosa*	Argan
Avocado	*Persea gratissima*	Avocat
Borage	*Borrago officinalis*	Bourrache
Castor	*Ricinus communis*	Ricin
Evening primrose	*Oenothera biennis*	Onagre
Grape seed	*Vitis vinifera*	Pépin de raisin
Hazelnut	*Corylus avellana*	Noisette
Hemp	*Cannabis sativa*	Chanvre
Jojoba	*Simmondsia chinensis*	Jojoba
Macadamia	*Macadamia integrifolia*	Macadamia
Musk rose/ rosehip seed	*Rosa rubiginosa/ R. mosqueta*	Rose musquée
Olive	*Olea europaea*	Olive
Sesame	*Sesamum indicum*	Sésame

Sunflower	*Helianthus annuus*	Tournesol
Sweet almond	*Prunus amygdalus*	Amande douce
Wheat germ	*Tricticum vulgare*	Germe de blé

EXOTIC VEGETABLE OILS

English	*Latin*	French
Babassu	*Orbignya barbosiana*	Babassu
Baobab	*Adansonia digitata*	Baobab
Camelina	*Camelina sativa*	Cameline
Camellia	*Camellia sinensis/ oleifera/japonica*	Camélia
Cranberry seed	*Vaccinium macrocarpon*	Pépins de canneberge
Karanja	*Pongamia glabra*	Karanja
Kukui	*Aleurites moluccana*	Kukui/Bancoule
Marula	*Sclerocarya birrea*	Marula
Meadowfoam	*Limnanthes alba*	Limnanthes
Neem	*Azadirachta indica*	Neem/Margousier
Nigella/black cumin	*Nigella sativa*	Nigelle/Cumin noir
Prickly pear/ cactus pear	*Opuntia ficus indica*	Figue de Barbarie
Raspberry seed	*Rubus idaeus*	Pépins de framboise
Rice bran	*Oryza sativa*	Son de riz
Sea buckthorn	*Hippophaë rhamnoides*	Argousier
Tamanu	*Calophyllum inophyllum*	Calophylle inophyle
Watermelon/ Kalahari melon seed	*Citrullus lanatus*	Melon du Kalahari

VEGETABLE BUTTERS

English	*Latin*	French
Cocoa	*Theobroma cacao*	Cacao
Coconut	*Cocos nucifera*	Noix de coco
Illipe	*Shorea stenoptera*	Illipé
Kokum	*Garcinia indica*	Kokum
Mango	*Mangifera indica*	Mangue
Sal	*Shorea robusta*	Sal
Shea	*Butyrospermum parkii*	Karité

INFUSED OILS

English	*Latin*	French
Calendula/marigold	*Calendula officinalis*	Calendula
Carrot	*Daucus carota var. sativa*	Carotte (cultivée)
Comfrey	*Symphytum officinale*	Consoude
Daisy	*Bellis perennis*	Pâquerette
English plantain	*Plantago lanceolata*	Plantain lancéolé/ Petit plantain
Greater plantain	*Plantago major*	Plantain majeur (à larges feuilles)
White lily	*Lilium candidum*	Lys blanc

ESSENTIAL OILS

English	*Latin*	French
Atlas Cedar	*Cedrus atlantica*	Cèdre de l'Atlas
Bay rum/ West Indian bay	*Pimenta racemosa*	Bay de St. Thomas

Benzoin/Siam	*Styrax Tonkinensis*	Benjoin
Black spruce	*Picea mariana*	Épinette noire
Blue tansy	*Tanacetum annuum*	Tanaisie annuelle
Carrot (wild)	*Daucus carota*	Carotte (sauvage)
Clary sage	*Salvia sclarea*	Sauge sclarée
Clove	*Syzgium aromaticum /Eugenia caryophyllus*	Clou de girofle
Celery	*Apium graveolens*	Céleri
Cypress	*Cupressus sempervirens*	Cyprès
Eastern Red Cedar/ virginian cedar	*Juniperus virginiana*	Genévrier de Virginie
Geranium/Rose geranium	*Pelargonium x asperum*	Géranium rosat
German/Blue chamomile	*Matricaria recutita*	Camomille allemande
Green myrtle	*Myrtus communis ct cineole*	Myrte vert
Helichrysum	*Helichrysum italicum*	Hélichryse
Himalayan Cedar	*Cedrus deodora*	Cèdre de l'Hhymalaya
Juniper	*Juniperus communis*	Genévrier commun
Laurel	*Laurus nobilis*	Laurier
Lemon eucalyptus	*Eucalyptus citriodora*	Eucalyptus citronné
Myrrh	*Commiphora myrrha/C. molmol*	Myrrhe
Neroli	*Citrus aurantium var. amara*	Néroli
Palmarosa	*Cymbopogon martinii*	Palmarosa

Patchouli	*Pogostemon cablin*	Patchouli
Peppermint	*Mentha x piperita*	Menthe poivrée
Peppermint eucalyptus ct Piperitone	*Eucalyptus dives ct piperitone*	Eucalyptus mentholé à pipéritone
Petitgrain bigarade	*Citrus aurantium var. amara*	Petit grain bigarade
Rock rose/ labdanum	*Cistus ladaniferus*	Ciste
Roman chamomile	*Chamaemelum nobile /Anthemis nobilis*	Camomille romaine
Rose	*Rosa damascena*	Rose
Rosemary ct verbenone	*Rosmarinus officinalis ct verbenoniferum*	Romarin à verbénone
Rosewood	*Aniba rosaeodora/ A. parviflora*	Bois de rose
Sandalwood	*Santalum album*	Bois de Santal
Sea fennel/ rock samphire	*Crithmum maritimum*	Criste-marine
Spearmint	*Mentha spicata*	Menthe verte/ M. douce
Spike lavender	*Lavandula latifolia spica*	Lavande aspic
Tea tree	*Melaleuca alternifolia*	Tea-tree/ Mélaleuque à feuilles alternées
True lavender	*Lavandula angustifolia/L. vera/L. officinalis*	Lavande vraie ou officinale
Ylang-ylang	*Cananga odorata var. genuina*	Ylang-ylang

HYDROSOLS

(other than those already listed under essential oils)		
English	*Latin*	**French**
Cornflower	*Centaurea cyanus*	Bleuet
Lemon balm/ Melissa	*Melissa officinalis*	Mélisse
Lemon verbena	*Aloysia citriodora/ Lippia citriodora*	Verveine odorante/ V. citronnée
Witch hazel	*Hamamelis virginiana*	Hamamélis
Yarrow	*Achillea millefolium*	Achillée millefeuille

Appendix 4: Latin Lexicon

CLASSIC VEGETABLE OILS

Latin	English	French
Argania spinosa	Argan/Argania	Argan
Borrago officinalis	Borage	Bourrache
Cannabis sativa	Hemp	Chanvre
Corylus avellana	Hazelnut	Noisette
Helianthus annuus	Sunflower	Tournesol
Macadamia integrifolia	Macadamia	Macadamia
Oenothera biennis	Evening primrose	Onagre
Olea europaea	Olive	Olive
Persea gratissima	Avocado	Avocat
Prunus amygdalus	Sweet almond	Amande douce
Prunus armeniaca	Apricot kernel	Noyau d'abricot
Ricinus communis	Castor	Ricin
Rosa rubiginosa/ R. mosqueta	Musk rose/ rosehip seed	Rose musquée

Sesamum indicum	Sesame	Sésame
Simmondsia chinensis	Jojoba	Jojoba
Tricticum vulgare	Wheat germ	Germe de blé
Vitis vinifera	Grape seed	Pépin de raisin

EXOTIC VEGETABLE OILS

Latin	**English**	**French**
Adansonia digitata	Baobab	Baobab
Aleurites moluccana	Kukui	Kukui/Bancoule
Azadirachta indica	Neem	Neem/Margousier
Calophyllum inophyllum	Tamanu	Calophylle inophyle
Camelina sativa	Camelina	Cameline
Camellia sinensis/ oleifera/japonica	Camellia	Camélia
Citrullus lanatus	Watermelon/ Kalahari melon seed	Melon du Kalahari
Hippophaë rhamnoides	Sea buckthorn	Argousier
Limnanthes alba	Meadowfoam	Limnanthes
Nigella sativa	Nigella/black cumin	Nigelle/Cumin noir
Opuntia ficus indica	Prickly pear/ cactus pear	Figue de Barbarie
Orbignya barbosiana	Babassu	Babassu
Oryza sativa	Rice bran	Son de riz
Pongamia glabra	Karanja	Karanja
Rubus idaeus	Raspberry seed	Pépins de framboise
Sclerocarya birrea	Marula	Marula
Vaccinium macrocarpon	Cranberry seed	Pépins de canneberge

VEGETABLE BUTTERS

Latin	English	French
Butyrospermum parkii	Shea	Karité
Cocos nucifera	Coconut	Noix de coco
Garcinia indica	Kokum	Kokum
Mangifera indica	Mango	Mangue
Shorea robusta	Sal	Sal
Shorea stenoptera	Illipe	Illipé
Theobroma cacao	Cocoa	Cacao

INFUSED OILS

Latin	English	French
Bellis perennis	Daisy	Pâquerette
Calendula officinalis	Calendula/marigold	Calendula
Daucus carota var. sativa	Carrot	Carotte (cultivée)
Lilium candidum	White lily	Lys blanc
Plantago lanceolata	English plantain	Plantain lancéolé/ Petit plantain
Plantago major	Greater plantain	Plantain majeur (à larges feuilles)
Symphytum officinale	Comfrey	Consoude

ESSENTIAL OILS

Latin	English	French
Aniba rosaeodora/ A. parviflora	Rosewood	Bois de rose
Apium graveolens	Celery	Céleri

Cananga odorata var. genuina	Ylang-ylang	Ylang-ylang
Cedrus atlantica	Atlas Cedar	Cèdre de l'Atlas
Cedrus deodora	Himalayan Cedar	Cèdre de l'Hymalaya
Chamaemelum nobile /Anthemis nobilis	Roman chamomile	Camomille romaine
Cistus ladaniferus	Rock rose/ labdanum	Ciste
Citrus aurantium var. amara	Petitgrain bigarade	Petit grain bigarade
Citrus aurantium var. amara	Neroli	Néroli
Commiphora myrrha/C. molmol	Myrrh	Myrrhe
Crithmum maritimum	Sea fennel/ rock samphire	Criste-marine
Cupressus sempervirens	Cypress	Cyprès
Cymbopogon martinii	Palmarosa	Palmarosa
Daucus carota	Carrot (wild)	Carotte (sauvage)
Eucalyptus citriodora	Lemon eucalyptus	Eucalyptus citronné
Eucalyptus dives ct piperitone	Peppermint eucalyptus ct piperitone	Eucalyptus mentholé à pipéritone
Helichrysum italicum	Helichrysum	Hélichryse
Juniperus virginiana	Eastern Red Cedar/ virginian cedar	Genévrier de Virginie
Juniperus communis	Juniper	Genévrier commun

Laurus nobilis	Laurel	Laurier
Lavandula angustifolia/L. vera/L. officinalis	True lavender	Lavande vraie ou officinale
Lavandula latifolia spica	Spike lavender	Lavande aspic
Matricaria recutita	German/Blue chamomile	Camomille allemande
Melaleuca alternifolia	Tea tree	Tea-tree/ Mélaleuque à feuilles alternées
Mentha spicata	Spearmint	Menthe verte/ M. douce
Mentha x piperita	Peppermint	Menthe poivrée
Myrtus communis ct cineole	Green myrtle	Myrte vert
Pelargonium x asperum	Geranium/Rose geranium	Géranium rosat
Picea mariana	Black spruce	Épinette noire
Pimenta racemosa	Bay rum/West Indian bay	Bay de St-Thomas
Pogostemon cablin	Patchouli	Patchouli
Rosa damascene	Rose	Rose
Rosmarinus officinalis ct verbenoniferum	Rosemary ct verbenone	Romarin à verbénone
Salvia sclarea	Clary sage	Sauge sclarée
Santalum album	Sandalwood	Bois de Santal
Styrax tonkinensis	Benzoin/Siam	Benjoin
Syzgium aromaticum/Eugenia caryophyllus	Clove	Clou de girofle
Tanacetum annuum	Blue tansy	Tanaisie annuelle

HYDROSOLS

(other than those already listed under essential oils)		
Latin	**English**	**French**
Achillea millefolium	Yarrow	Achillée millefeuilles
Aloysia citriodora/ Lippia citriodora	Lemon verbena	Verveine odorante/ V. citronnée
Centaurea cyanus	Cornflower	Bleuet
Hamamelis virginiana	Witch hazel	Hamamélis
Melissa officinalis	Lemon balm/ Melissa	Mélisse

Appendix 5: French Lexicon

CLASSIC VEGETABLE OILS

French	English	*Latin*
Amande douce	Sweet almond	*Prunus amygdalus*
Argan	Argan/Argania	*Argania spinosa*
Avocat	Avocado	*Persea gratissima*
Bourrache	Borage	*Borrago officinalis*
Chanvre	Hemp	*Cannabis sativa*
Germe de blé	Wheat germ	*Tricticum vulgare*
Jojoba	Jojoba	*Simmondsia chinensis*
Macadamia	Macadamia	*Macadamia integrifolia*
Noisette	Hazelnut	*Corylus avellana*
Noyau d'abricot	Apricot kernel	*Prunus armeniaca*
Olive	Olive	*Olea europaea*
Onagre	Evening primrose	*Oenothera biennis*
Pépin de raisin	Grape seed	*Vitis vinifera*

Ricin	Castor	*Ricinus communis*
Rose musquée	Musk rose/ rosehip seed	*Rosa rubiginosa/ R. mosqueta*
Sésame	Sesame	*Sesamum indicum*
Tournesol	Sunflower	*Helianthus annuus*

EXOTIC VEGETABLE OILS

French	**English**	***Latin***
Argousier	Sea buckthorn	*Hippophaë rhamnoides*
Babassu	Babassu	*Orbignya barbosiana*
Baobab	Baobab	*Adansonia digitata*
Calophylle inophyle	Tamanu	*Calophyllum inophyllum*
Cameline	Camelina	*Camelina sativa*
Camélia	Camellia	*Camellia sinensis/ oleifera/japonica*
Figue de Barbarie	Prickly pear/ cactus pear	*Opuntia ficus indica*
Karanja	Karanja	*Pongamia glabra*
Kukui/Bancoule	Kukui	*Aleurites moluccana*
Limnanthes	Meadowfoam	*Limnanthes alba*
Marula	Marula	*Sclerocarya birrea*
Melon du Kalahari	Watermelon/ Kalahari melon seed	*Citrullus lanatus*
Neem/Margousier	Neem	*Azadirachta indica*
Nigelle/Cumin noir	Nigella/black cumin	*Nigella sativa*
Pépins de canneberge	Cranberry seed	*Vaccinium macrocarpon*
Pépins de framboise	Raspberry seed	*Rubus idaeus*
Son de riz	Rice bran	*Oryza sativa*

VEGETABLE BUTTERS

French	English	Latin
Cacao	Cocoa	*Theobroma cacao*
Illipé	Illipe	*Shorea stenoptera*
Karité	Shea	*Butyrospermum parkii*
Kokum	Kokum	*Garcinia indica*
Mangue	Mango	*Mangifera indica*
Noix de coco	Coconut	*Cocos nucifera*
Sal	Sal	*Shorea robusta*

INFUSED OILS

French	English	Latin
Calendula	Calendula/marigold	*Calendula officinalis*
Carotte (cultivée)	Carrot	*Daucus carota var. sativa*
Consoude	Comfrey	*Symphytum officinale*
Lys blanc	White lily	*Lilium candidum*
Pâquerette	Daisy	*Bellis perennis*
Plantain lancéolé/ Petit plantain	English plantain	*Plantago lanceolata*
Plantain majeur (à larges feuilles)	Greater plantain	*Plantago major*

ESSENTIAL OILS

French	English	Latin
Bay de St-Thomas	Bay rum/ West Indian bay	*Pimenta racemosa*
Benjoin	Benzoin/Siam	*Styrax tonkinensis*

Bois de rose	Rosewood	*Aniba rosaeodora/A. parviflora*
Bois de Santal	Sandalwood	*Santalum album*
Camomille allemande	German/Blue chamomile	*Matricaria recutita*
Camomille romaine	Roman chamomile	*Chamaemelum nobile /Anthemis nobilis*
Carotte (sauvage)	Carrot (wild)	*Daucus carota*
Céleri	Celery	*Apium graveolens*
Cèdre de l'Atlas	Atlas Cedar	*Cedrus atlantica*
Cèdre de l'Hhymalaya	Himalayan Cedar	*Cedrus deodora*
Ciste	Rock rose/ labdanum	*Cistus ladaniferus*
Clou de girofle	Clove	*Syzgium aromaticum /Eugenia caryophyllus*
Criste-marine	Sea fennel/ rock samphire	*Crithmum maritimum*
Cyprès	Cypress	*Cupressus sempervirens*
Épinette noire	Black spruce	*Picea mariana*
Eucalyptus citronné	Lemon eucalyptus	*Eucalyptus citriodora*
Eucalyptus mentholé à pipéritone	Peppermint eucalyptus ct piperitone	*Eucalyptus dives ct piperitone*
Genévrier de Virginie	Eastern Red Cedar/ virginian cedar	*Juniperus virginiana*
Genévrier commun	Juniper	*Juniperus communis*
Géranium rosat	Geranium/ Rose geranium	*Pelargonium x asperum*

Hélichryse	Helichrysum	*Helichrysum italicum*
Laurier	Laurel	*Laurus nobilis*
Lavande aspic	Spike lavender	*Lavandula latifolia spica*
Lavande vraie ou officinale	True lavender	*Lavandula angustifolia/ L. vera/L. officinalis*
Menthe poivrée	Peppermint	*Mentha x piperita*
Menthe verte/M. douce	Spearmint	*Mentha spicata*
Myrrhe	Myrrh	*Commiphora myrrha/C. molmol*
Myrte vert	Green myrtle	*Myrtus communis ct cineole*
Néroli	Neroli	*Citrus aurantium var. amara*
Palmarosa	Palmarosa	*Cymbopogon martinii*
Patchouli	Patchouli	*Pogostemon cablin*
Petit grain bigarade	Petitgrain bigarade	*Citrus aurantium var. amara*
Romarin à verbénone	Rosemary ct verbenone	*Rosmarinus officinalis ct verbenoniferum*
Rose	Rose	*Rosa damascena*
Sauge sclarée	Clary sage	*Salvia sclarea*
Tanaisie annuelle	Blue tansy	*Tanacetum annuum*
Tea-tree/ Mélaleuque à feuilles alternées	Tea tree	*Melaleuca alternifolia*
Ylang-ylang	Ylang-ylang	*Cananga odorata var. genuina*

HYDROSOLS

(other than those already listed under essential oils)		
French	**English**	*Latin*
Achillée millefeuille	Yarrow	*Achillea millefolium*
Bleuet	Cornflower	*Centaurea cyanus*
Hamamélis	Witch hazel	*Hamamelis virginiana*
Mélisse	Lemon Balm/ Melissa	*Melissa officinalis*
Verveine odorante/ V. citronnée	Lemon verbena	*Aloysia citriodora/ Lippia citriodora*

Glossary

Acne: an inflammatory condition of the sebaceous glands and hair follicles of the skin due to various causes. It is marked by the eruption of pimples, particularly on the face, upper chest, and back. The ingredients presented in this book can alleviate the symptoms of acne, but it is highly recommended to consult a physician in the case of severe acne.

Allergies: hypersensitivity of the immune system to normally harmless substances. The ingredients presented in this book can alleviate the symptoms of a skin allergy, but it is highly recommended not to use essential oils and to consult a physician in the case of a severe allergy.

Analgesic: helps reduce the feeling of pain. Anti-allergic: helps alleviate allergic reactions.

Antibacterial: prevents and combats the growth of bacteria.

Anticoagulant: helps increase the fluidity the blood.

Antifungal: prevents and combats fungal infection.

Anti-inflammatory: helps reduce inflammation (a painful redness or swelling of the skin).

Antioxidant: helps prevent or delay the oxidation or deterioration of the skin cells.

Antiperspirant: helps control the production of perspiration by the body.

Antipigmentation: helps reduce pigmentation spots that usually appear with age on the back of the hands, the face, and the shoulders.

Antiseborrheic: helps control the production of sebum, the oily secretion of the skin.

Antiseptic: helps destroy and prevent the growth of microbes (bacteria, virus, and fungus).

Antiviral: prevents and combats the growth of a virus.

Astringent: causes the contraction of the skin and the pores.

Blackheads: tiny black spots on the skin of the face and shoulders caused by the accumulation of sebum and dead skin cells in the opening of a skin follicle. They are also called comedones.

Brittle: hair, usually dry, that breaks easily due to excessive sun exposure, chlorine from swimming pools, overuse of some products, salon treatments, poor diet, or other causes. Nail that breaks easily.

Bruise: an injury, usually caused by a blunt impact, in which the skin is not broken but the capillaries are damaged, allowing blood to seep into the surrounding tissue, leaving a temporary bluish, purplish mark.

Burn: light burn usually results in local redness of the skin and sometimes a blister. The ingredients presented in this book can alleviate the symptoms of a light burn, but it is highly recommended to consult a physician in the case of a more severe or extended burn.

Calming: helps reduce the unpleasant sensations of irritated skin (itching, burning, etc.).

Cellulite: fatty deposit in the skin causing an uneven appearance and texture (cottage-cheese-like).

Chapped: skin that is dry, cracked, and sore.

Chemotype (ct): the specific composition of an essential oil that has been extracted from a particular plant. This plant can yield essential oils with different aromatic molecules according to the condition (altitude, climate, light, etc.) in which it grew. For example, "Rosemary ct (for chemotype) verbenone" means that this essential oil has a high amount of the chemical molecule called verbenone.

Circulatory: contributes to improving the circulation of blood and then helps reduce troubles such as varicose veins or couperosis.

Clarifying: helps get a brighter complexion.

Coagulant: helps stop the bleeding of a wound or a cut.

Cold sores (labial herpes): a viral infection responsible for painful inflammation spots on the lips, often combined with clusters of deep-seated vesicles (fluid-filled blisters).

Couperosis: a skin condition due to weak, small blood vessels (capillaries) and inflammation. This condition is also called spider veins. It usually affects the nose and the cheeks. It must not be confused with rosacea, which is a different skin condition.

Cultivar (cv): designates a plant that has been deliberately selected for its specificity; in this case, its particular components.

Damaged: damaged skin has scars or signs of premature aging. Damaged hair usually lacks shine and strength. It often presents split ends and breakage.

Dandruff: white flakes of dead skin that shed from the scalp, due to overworking of sebaceous glands of the scalp or to a fungus, among other causes.

Dark circles: a more or less intense, dark bluish-purple coloration of the skin around the eyes. They are due to a slow, visible microcirculation of the blood in the soft skin of this area. They can be inherited or the result of a lack of sleep or of various health conditions.

Decongestant: helps reduce the swelling of the skin.

Deodorizing: helps destroy the bacteria responsible for body odors.

Dilated pores: natural small openings of the skin that have enlarged and become visible.

Dry: skin that does not have enough moisture. It is due to a reduced production of sebum by the sebaceous gland. It usually makes the skin or the scalp irritated and itchy, sometimes flaky and more wrinkled. Dry hair is brittle and hard to brush.

Dull hair: hair that lacks shine, strength, and vitality.

Eczema: a medical condition that makes your skin itch and become rough and sore. Some of the ingredients presented in this book can alleviate the symptoms of eczema, but it is highly recommended to consult a physician if the condition is severe.

Epilepsy: a disorder of the central nervous system characterized by loss of consciousness and convulsions.

Excessive perspiration: an excessive production of sweat through the pores of the skin by the sweat glands.

Fine hair: thin hair that usually lacks strength and body.

Firming: helps tighten the skin and tissues, thus reducing wrinkles and sagging.

Fragile: skin is more fragile around the neck and the eyes. There it tends to wrinkle earlier and more easily.

Fungal infection: a skin condition due to a fungus. Some of the ingredients presented in this book can alleviate the symptoms of a fungal infection, but it is highly recommended to consult a physician if the condition is severe.

Hair loss: falling out of the hair that is more significant than it should normally be and produces a thinning of the hair on the scalp.

Healing: helps restore skin damage by small wounds, abrasions, and so on.

Hormone-dependent cancer: a cancer (breast, ovary, uterus, prostate), the growth of which is or may be stimulated by the sex hormones.

Hydrating: helps to keep or add water or moisture to the skin, and then contributes to toning and maintaining its firmness.

Insecticide, insectifuge: helps kill insects or repel them.

Irritated: an itchy, reddish skin. This can come from many causes.

Lavandin: Lavandin is a hybrid between true lavender and spike lavender. Its EO is of less aromatic, therapeutic, and price values. (The large fields cultivated in Provence are usually lavandin.) For some uses (as an insectifuge, for example) it is cheaper, with the same effect as true lavender.

Mature: a mature skin is thinner, drier, more wrinkled, and more spotted than the skin of a young person.

Mixed: a mixed skin shows some parts of the face that are oily, usually the T-Zone (nose, forehead, and chin) and others that are dry (cheeks).

Nourishing: contributes to give to the skin what it needs to stay in good shape and health. Remember that the skin (and the hair) is primarily maintained and nourished by the nutritive substances delivered by the blood.

Oily: skin or scalp is oily when there is an excessive production of sebum by the sebaceous gland. The skin or the hair looks and feels greasy.

Photosensitivity: an increased sensitivity of the skin to the sunlight. Some essential oils can cause photosensitivity, resulting in redness, hyperpigmentation of the skin, even permanent skin-cell damage.

Pigmentation spots: dark, irregular spots that appear on the skin due to age, long-term sun exposure, or other causes. They occur when an excess of melanin forms deposits in the skin.

Protective: keeps the skin safe from damage inflicted by elements such as sun or wind.

Psoriasis: a medical condition due to the overly rapid growth of the skin cells that accumulate on the skin surface, forming raised, red patches or lesions. The exact cause of this disease is still unknown. The ingredients presented in this book can alleviate the symptoms of psoriasis, but it is highly recommended to consult a physician in the case of a severe condition.

Purifying: helps bring impurities to the surface of the skin and unblock the pores.

Refreshing: makes the skin feel cooler.

Regenerating: helps renew and rejuvenate the skin and then contribute to improving it, especially if it is dull or aging.

Sallow complexion: a pale yellowish complexion that looks unhealthy.

Scar: a mark left on the skin after a surface injury or a wound or a lesion has healed.

Sensitive: a sensitive skin is prone to redness, blotchiness, and irritation due to many causes, including chemicals, fluctuations of temperature, and sun exposure.

Slimming: helps to eliminate fat under the skin, such as cellulite, and then to stay thinner.

Softening: makes the skin smoother and pleasant to touch.

Soothing: helps reduce the unpleasant sensations of irritated skin (itching, burning, etc.).

Strengthening: helps get hair, nails, or eyelashes stronger so they break less easily.

Stretch marks: tears in the dermis, also called stria. They look like shiny lines on the skin of the abdomen, breasts, thighs, or buttocks caused by the prolonged stretching of the skin and weakening of elastic tissues, as in pregnancy or obesity.

Sunscreen: some ingredients in this book contain natural sunscreens and help to protect the skin from the damage caused by the sun. They generally have a sun protection factor (SPF) equal to or less than 5, which is not sufficient for long exposure to full summer sun.

Supple (more): helps to make skin soft and not crack or feel tight, as, for example, chapped skin usually does.

Thymol: Thymol is an aromatic molecule that is very anti-infectious, but irritating for the skin.

Toning: helps tighten the skin and tissues and then reduces wrinkles and sagging. Gives more strength to the hair.

Varicose vein: a vein that is permanently dilated. It is common on legs.

Wound: a light wound of the skin can be a cut or a scratch. The ingredients presented in this book can alleviate the symptoms of a light wound, but it is highly recommended to consult a physician in the case of a more severe wound.

Wrinkled: skin that has lines or creases, generally due to age. It usually appears on mature skin.

Bibliography

Baudoux, Dominique. *L'aromathérapie: se soigner par les huiles essentielles.* Anglet, France: Éditions Atlantica, 2001.

Baudoux, Dominique, and Abdesselam Zhiri. *Les cahiers pratiques d'aromathérapie selon l'école française, Volume 2: dermatologie.* Luxembourg: Éditions Inspir, 2003.

Catty, Suzanne. *Hydrosols: The Next Aromatherapy.* Rochester, VT: Healing Arts Press, 2001.

Chevalier, Andrew. *Encyclopédie des plantes médicinales.* Montréal: Sélection Reader's Digest, 1996.

Clergeaud, Chantal. *Votre beauté au naturel: comment préparer vous-même tous vos produits de beauté.* Saint-Jean-de-Braye, France: Éditions Dangles, 2002.

Clergeaud, Chantal, and Lionel Clergeaud. *Les huiles végétales: Huiles de beauté et de santé.* Biarritz, France: Éditions Atlantica, 2000.

Franchomme, Pierre, and Daniel Pénoël. *L'aromathérapie exactement: Encyclopédie de l'utilisation thérapeutique des huiles essentielles.* Limoges, France: Éditions Roger Jollois, 2001.

Lavédrine, Anne. *Les bienfaits des huiles.* Neuilly-sur-Seine, France: Éditions Michel Lafon, 2001.

Lawless, Julia. *The Encyclopedia of Essential Oils: The Complete Guide to the Use of Aromatic Oils in Aromatherapy, Herbalism, Health and Well-being.* London: Thorsons, 2002.

Pénoël, Daniel. *Médecine aromatique, médecine planétaire: vers la fin d'une survie artificielle.* Limoges, France: Éditions Roger Jollois, 1991.

Price, Len, and Shirley Price. *Understanding Hydrolats: The Specific Hydrosols for Aromatherapy: A Guide for Health Professionals.* London: Churchill Livingstone, 2004.

Roulier, Guy. *Les huiles essentielles pour votre santé. Traité pratique d'aromathérapie: propriétés et indications des essences de plantes.* Saint-Jean-de-Braye, France: Éditions Dangles, 1990.

Schnaubelt, Kurt. *Advanced Aromatherapy: The Science of Essential Oil Therapy.* Rochester, VT: Healing Arts Press, 1998.

Stiens, Rita. *La vérité sur les cosmétiques.* Paris: Presses du management, 2001; Leduc Éditions, 2005.

Zhiri, Abdesselam, and Dominique Baudoux. *H.E.T.C. — Huiles essentielles chémotypées et leurs synergies.* Brussels: Éditions Amyris, 2002.

Index

TO WRITE TO THE AUTHOR

If you wish to contact the author or would like more information about this book, please write to the author in care of Llewellyn Worldwide Ltd. and we will forward your request. Both the author and the publisher appreciate hearing from you and learning of your enjoyment of this book and how it has helped you. Llewellyn Worldwide Ltd. cannot guarantee that every letter written to the author can be answered, but all will be forwarded. Please write to:

Hélène Berton
⅟ Llewellyn Worldwide
2143 Wooddale Drive
Woodbury, MN 55125-2989

Please enclose a self-addressed stamped envelope for reply, or $1.00 to cover costs. If outside the U.S.A., enclose an international postal reply coupon.

GET MORE AT LLEWELLYN.COM

Visit us online to browse hundreds of our books and decks, plus
sign up to receive our e-newsletters and exclusive online offers.

- **Free tarot readings • Spell-a-Day • Moon phases**
- **Recipes, spells, and tips • Blogs • Encyclopedia**
- **Author interviews, articles, and upcoming events**

GET SOCIAL WITH LLEWELLYN

Find us on Facebook
www.Facebook.com/LlewellynBooks

Follow us on

www.Twitter.com/Llewellynbooks

GET BOOKS AT LLEWELLYN

LLEWELLYN ORDERING INFORMATION

Order online: Visit our website at www.llewellyn.com to select your books
and place an order on our secure server.

Order by phone:
- Call toll free within the U.S. at 1-877-NEW-WRLD (1-877-639-9753)
- Call toll free within Canada at 1-866-NEW-WRLD (1-866-639-9753)
- We accept VISA, MasterCard, and American Express

Order by mail:
Send the full price of your order (MN residents add 6.875% sales tax) in U.S. funds,
plus postage and handling to: Llewellyn Worldwide, 2143 Wooddale Drive
Woodbury, MN 55125-2989

POSTAGE AND HANDLING

STANDARD (U.S. & Canada):
(Please allow 12 business days)
$25.00 and under, add $4.00.
$25.01 and over, FREE SHIPPING.

INTERNATIONAL ORDERS (airmail only):
$16.00 for one book, plus $3.00 for
each additional book.

Visit us online for more shipping options.
Prices subject to change.

FREE CATALOG!

To order, call
1-877-
NEW-WRLD
ext. 8236
or visit our
website